Diana   *May, 2016*

LIVE TO LEAD

THE MISSING LINK IN
LEADERSHIP DEVELOPMENT

So pleased to see the evolution of CHF under your leadership. Keep going/growing.

Wayne Stewart

WAYNE STEWART

Suite 300 - 990 Fort St
Victoria, BC, Canada, V8V 3K2
www.friesenpress.com

ISBN
978-1-4602-8546-6 (Hardcover)
978-1-4602-8547-3 (Paperback)
978-1-4602-8548-0 (eBook)

1. Business & Economics, Leadership

Distributed to the trade by The Ingram Book Company

DEDICATION

Dedicated to all those who seek understanding, especially those embarking on their life work on whose leadership rests our hope.

ACKNOWLEDGMENTS

So many friends have contributed to whatever success I have had in life and in leadership that I hesitate to name some and miss many more. I do want to offer a special thanks to three among the many.

Danielle Gibbie, a delightful young woman just beginning to make what will be an enormous contribution, reviewed an early draft and encouraged me to publish. Steve Armstrong, author, speaker, coach and all round good guy, offered advice on the creative aspects of the book that was most helpful. Ruben Nelson, executive director of Foresight Canada, has consistently challenged me to do more and his urging initiated the project in the first instance.

Beyond that, to my many friends, know that your counsel along the journey is greatly appreciated.

BOOKS BY WAYNE STEWART

Citizenship in the 21st Century- Lessons from the present

Things I Know- Bits of wisdom for leaders of non-profits and others, in my own voice

Reflections on a Campaign

TABLE OF CONTENTS

BEFORE WE START

"If ever leadership was needed", a cliché repeated endlessly, as relevant now as ever.

In a world of chaos where the gap, in the west, between expectations and reality is so enormous, the cry goes out once again. In a world gone beyond mad- consumption patterns unsustainable even in the short term, economic turmoil of a magnitude beyond the experience of all but the very old, uncertainty and instability on all fronts, and the ever present threat of terrorist harm, where, we wonder, are those who will lead us into a future of promise and hope?

As we search for leadership, we very often turn to those with a record of success in the corporate sector, the heroes of our time. Yet we wonder, is this the appropriate source? Indeed, are we using the correct measure of success? Do these corporate 'giants' have the right stuff, the background, the knowledge and skills, and most importantly, the right attitude and approach to provide the leadership needed at this critical time? Does the fact of personal success as we measure it (million dollar salaries, multiple homes and other measures of personal wealth and unlimited consumption ability and practice) ensure leadership abilities in such times as now experienced?

Do the assumptions that have pervaded thinking on leadership (as examples, the link between senior management position and leadership ability, the notion that leadership must come from the top, the acceptance that MBA education prepares one for leadership) any longer hold? Might it be better to seek leaders from the public sector, from government or the bureaucracy (bound to be some risk here as well)? Are there people in the non profit world who might play larger leadership roles (a source not yet extensively tested)?

1

Perhaps what is at issue is the very essence of leadership. What is this concept that we want to call leadership and what should we expect of those who fill the role? Given many recent examples of failed leadership, might the problem lie in how we prepare for a leadership role, in the backgrounds we seek, the education we provide, the routes available for experience and the models and heroes we hold up? How do we ensure that leaders approach their role with the appropriate attitude?

> **Perhaps what is at issue is the very essence of leadership.**

This work was undertaken as a response to a number of overlapping concerns. First and perhaps most important is the leadership vacuum so apparent today. Adding to and exacerbating this lack of leadership is an inappropriate approach taken by so many of those to whom we assign the role of leader. An inescapable conclusion is that something in their background, education and/or experience must have been missing. Perhaps the process of identifying, developing and assigning people to leadership roles is flawed.

The logic of the work is that the first step as preparation for leadership, a step largely missing from current literature and leadership teaching, is a thorough understanding of self. Leadership is about 'being' as against 'doing'. To be leader, one must be aware of self, of who he/she is at a deep and fundamental level. A failure to 'be', with all that attends, will ultimately result, at best, in reduced contribution in the leadership role, and in the worst case, to complete failure and the attendant personal crises that so often follow, for both the leader and those whom he/she would lead.

As one deepens the search for an answer to the "who am I?" question, they prepare themselves for the best life as they enhance their leadership capacity. Live to Lead- preparation for Life prepares you for Leadership. In all cases, Life must come first for best performance as Leader.

A second important area, also largely avoided by authors and teachers in the leadership arena, is the 'love' dimension. As one becomes increasingly aware of whom they really are, self love emerges. From this base, the very essence of love becomes part of the person's being, affecting their approach to people and tasks, inseparable from whom they have become.

With awareness of self and love as background, the responsibility to lead becomes evident as one observes the need and an irresistible urge emerges to fill that need, out of love. Deep self awareness provides the personal balance and protection required to continue to contribute at a high level in the midst of the huge responsibility that attends with the leadership role.

Much has been written about leadership. One can also find lots of books on love in bookstore self-help sections. What has been missing in current literature is the critical nature of self awareness. This present work has been undertaken largely to address this missing element and will focus on self awareness, onto which the writing of many others, more qualified than myself, on the topics of love and leadership can be mapped.

So, with an introduction and a bit more context, let us begin.

LIVE TO LEAD:

An introduction

Those who, like me, are regular visitors to book stores in search of new ideas and novel concepts, find a multitude of books on leadership, a discipline that would seem in continual evolution (turmoil might be a better word) as evidenced by the number of books on the topic. Yet even those with 'Leadership' in the title are most often displayed within a section on Business Management or Economics, indicative of a misperception that leadership is the purview of managers and suggestive of the importance of economic education to a role as leader.

The content promised by book titles, cover flap summaries, and indeed a thorough 'read' covers a range of leadership theories and models, often incorporated within biographical information of leader so-and-so. Most of the 'so-and-so's' are those who have achieved success in business, very often measured by growth of personal wealth and/or their ability to cut costs, restructure the company and improve share value. In many, many cases, the resultant impact on the ordinary company employee has been negative.

> **Management is about efficiency and control and focuses mainly on the short term; leadership is about vision, inspiration and empowerment with a long term focus.**

Much of the literature on leadership is, in reality, heavily slanted toward management theory, role and skills. While not devaluing the importance of sound management, leadership must be seen as a distinct discipline. To subsume leadership under the management umbrella is to both devalue the concept and contribute to the leadership gap that already exists. Management is about efficiency and control and focuses mainly on the short term; leadership is about vision, inspiration and empowerment with a long term focus. To lead with only management skills and approaches often produces solid results in the short term at the expense of long term success.

Experience suggests that even the best books on leadership fall short in at least three areas. First, attention to the critical role of self awareness is inadequate. While certain models suggest self awareness as either the place to start (as one example, see Goleman's work on Emotional Intelligence) or as one of a number of characteristics of leaders (Greenleaf's concept of servant leadership), in all cases, much more is required to emphasize the importance and to help people find their way to self.

A second shortfall is the avoidance of the concept of love as a guiding principle for leaders; even the word evokes negative reactions from hard-nosed business people. Lance Secretan introduces the word and the concept in his work on Higher Ground Leaders but even here the concept is not fully fleshed out (and he is pretty much alone in using the highly charged word in a text designed for a business audience).

Like love, spirituality as a learning discipline is missing from leadership texts. Much can be learned through spiritual processes which are particularly helpful in a search for self awareness. The concept of spirituality and its role in leadership development is absented even more completely than love.

In a way, these shortfalls are understandable given that the texts are written to be sold. The 'market' for such books lies largely in the private sector where these concepts are foreign, frightening and unacceptable to private sector folks and their inclusion is likely to affect sales in a negative way. The term used to describe these concepts, 'fuzz', is anathema to senior managers who want to be seen as decisive, efficient and 'hard'. Yet there is ample evidence that only as we discover self are we able to live fully. Love emerges then, first of self and then of others. Finally, the need for leadership becomes obvious; we see and accept the responsibility to lead and we are equipped to do so. Love emerges from self awareness and leadership from love. To lead fully effectively, one must attend to self awareness and learn to love.

While solid literature is available on the three concepts identified as lacking in business books, it is found in the book store in sections on self help, psychology and religion, all places that business people avoid (for fear of being seen and then forever categorized as soft). It strikes me as interesting that we get an equivalent reaction from religious groups who reject lessons from business and avoid business literature for fear of contamination ("we don't want to appear hard").

Leadership suffers from a series of false assumptions about the concept. In my early private sector work, I learned that management had four functions, one of which was leading. This naturally fed an assumption that only managers can lead, resulting in a terrible shortage of leadership and an impossible burden on managers. We have also been told that leadership is an inherent ability, one which you are born either with or without.

These assumptions affect our educational approach which emphasizes management as against leadership. The highly valued MBA programs stress techniques and skills appropriate to managing and often anathema to leading. Where leadership is promised by course title, content very often devolves to management issues and approaches. A recent educational experience provided a concrete example of the inadequacy of leadership training as the role of leader as transformative agent was emphasized in the complete absence of any help in how that was to be effected. Graduates are sent into their careers with a mission to transform (a useful leadership role) and no understanding of what is required to do so.

I have written this book to address the shortcomings observed in current literature on leadership with a particular focus on self awareness, the foundation for the best life and success as leader. My prime objective is to enhance understanding of the essence of leadership as the missing elements are addressed. My hope is that the experience on which the book is based is helpful to a broad audience, including those who would provide leadership in all walks of life, in the corporate world, in the public sector and in community work.

I have been working in the leadership arena for over 30 years. In the early part of that period, as a senior manager in the private sector, I was involved in some of the early work on corporate mission, visioning and strategic transformation. In the early 1990s, I taught leadership to graduating MBA students, starting from the base of self awareness. In the mid 1990s, I became aware of the work of Robert Greenleaf on servant leadership and have been a practitioner and a huge fan ever since. In three senior positions in the non profit sector, I have practiced leadership in situations that called for strategic change and transformation. More recently, my partner, Corey Olynik and I developed and implemented a highly successful coaching process for non profit sector leaders, once again starting from self awareness as foundation.

All along the way, I have continued my own search for self through a series of approaches which have helped me to an improved understanding of who I am while improving my ability to lead as evident by success of the organizations and people who have looked to me for leadership. At the same time, the more thorough my understanding of self has become, the better has been my life apart from any leadership role. The impact on my apparent ability and the coincident contribution to the other parts of my life have convinced me of the critical nature of self awareness as the starting point of any process designed to enhance life and improve leadership, both so sorely needed at any time.

This focus on self awareness as foundation for life and leadership is the unique element in my approach to development of leadership capacity. Accordingly, that is the focus of the book. Building on an understanding of self, a chapter on integration with life role is suggested as a route to a happy life and maximum contribution.

Also included is a short chapter of the Logic of Love. So much literature is available on leadership that little else needs to be said. I would encourage you to study the literature on servant leadership, the approach that I have found most relevant today.

The focus of the book, the critical nature of self awareness, demands that the content be largely quite serious. In order to provide some balance and to give a break from the seriousness, I have included some of my earlier writings that have contributed to growing awareness and from time to time have provided a chuckle. I leave it to you to ponder the lessons from each of these and to reflect on what they have contributed to who I am. The main point though is to encourage you to write and learn from your own stories, serious and funny.

At the end of each chapter, I have added some comments and questions to facilitate your journey to self awareness and stimulate further learning and leadership development. The final chapter is included to wrap the learning in a couple of enduring questions.

My hope is that this work makes a contribution to a more complete understanding of the essence of leadership and ultimately to the development of people equipped to lead in the chaos that characterizes the times. May it be so.

LIVE TO LEAD:

A Bit More Context

A friend of mine who has consulted in leadership for several years told me she has identified over three hundred definitions of leadership. Every author who writes on leadership offers their own, often a variation on a theme with a twist that they hope makes their definition unique and all-encompassing.

I make a habit of reading everything that I encounter on leadership. While I gain some new insight from almost everything that I read, I hold that the best sources, and the ones that have guided my practice of leadership, are the work of James Kouzes and Barry Posner and the entire body of work on Servant Leadership, including the original work of Robert Greenleaf (see www.greenleaf.org).

In their classic work, "The Leadership Challenge", Kouzes and Posner identify five practices of leaders as: model the way; challenge the process; inspire a shared vision; enable others to act; and encourage the heart.

In a delightful little book simply titled "The Servant Leader", James Autry outlines five ways of being that characterize servant leaders. Autry says that servant leaders must: "be authentic; be vulnerable; be accepting; be present; and be useful".

As I lead and as I coach others into leadership roles, I believe that the five practices and the five ways of being define a leader's role and the way he/she must 'be' in that role for best results. It is in the area of being, so essential to servant leadership, that self awareness is particularly critical. The remainder of this current work is offered within this context.

The suggestions offered have been effective in my work with aspiring leaders from a variety of age groups. In the constant barrage of information that characterizes our current times and the lowered attention span that has resulted in part from technology that requires short, snappy communication, I wonder whence leaders will emerge.

Development of leadership skills requires that one pay attention to the evolution of leadership theory over an extended period of time. The alternative is that leadership may simply revert to the trait approach which posits that leaders are born and only those who have the proper characteristics (some of these are merely physical) can ever aspire to lead. Trait theory of leadership has largely been replaced by theories that hold that leadership skills can be developed, that leaders are 'made' rather than born and that any who aspire to a role as leader can develop the required skills. I hold with these later theories.

I have tried to make this book appealing to those who suffer from this constant technological barrage by making the chapters short. However, at some level, two things are of particular importance if one is to learn to lead. First, one must pay attention to the messages that emerge from all learning opportunities, and second, an aspirant must take the time required to let the messages sink in. The need for leadership continues to be vitally important in a world characterized by so many huge issues, a time where deep understanding of our essential human nature is essential if we are to live and lead well.

THE FIRST STEP:

(the missing link): LIVE

"Some time when the river is ice, ask me mistakes I have made.
Ask me if what I have done is my life."

William Stafford, "Ask Me."

CHAPTER 1:

Who Am I? Initial Thoughts

I must live before I can love; I must love before I can lead.

The foundation for life, for love and for leadership is self awareness.

Bold statements, perhaps, but the messages of both are absolutely critical for success in life and in leadership. While many to whom authority on leadership is ascribed today allude to self awareness as an element of leadership (Greenleaf, for example, includes it in a list of 'ten characteristics'), in all cases, the concept is presented more or less as an afterthought to the main body of the work, an aside. Literature on leadership fails to point the reader to the critical importance of understanding self at a deep, fundamental level.

Harrison Owen's little book, *"Leadership Is"*, was an early attempt to help business leaders understand the importance of 'being' to leadership. I found Owen's approach of value in teaching leadership in the early 1990s where the students helped me understand that 'leadership is being' as contrasted against 'management is doing'.

1

James Autry, in *"The Servant Leader"*, identifies five ways of being important to servant leadership. The very first of these is 'being authentic.' Obviously, this requires a thorough knowledge of self. I simply cannot be authentically 'who I am' unless I first have answered the question 'who am I?'

Later efforts by Owen and others delved into the contribution of spirituality but seemed to have left the self behind, to the detriment of leadership development in the most profound and effective sense.

Warren Bennis has rightly pointed out that "becoming a leader is synonymous with becoming yourself. It is precisely that simple and it is also that difficult."

We cannot become all we might be without first understanding the starting point, who we are right now. Self awareness initiates the process of becoming, a life long journey. As we engage in the process of becoming leader, the only place to start is knowledge of self.

Experience has proven beyond doubt to me, both in personal leadership roles and in helping others develop their ability, that the starting point for best performance as leader is self awareness. This is entirely logical considering the link between life and leadership. Those who avoid the concept may have been influenced by the separation that so pervades modern thinking between one's work life and that part of life outside of work. It has long been clear, and is increasingly so, that this is a faulty separation, that to be best at work requires that we be best beyond work, that life is an integrated whole that cannot be separated into smaller bits without a negative impact on each of the bits.

Self awareness makes so many other things in our life work. Very often when we discover a failing in life and/or leadership, we attack the failing and avoid looking beyond to the underlying cause (a common approach on many fronts in our times where the solution must be identified and action taken quickly- it is more important that we act immediately than that we do the right thing if that takes time for reflection when we could have been acting). When the failure appears to be a lack of self confidence, for example, our immediate reaction is to send the leader to a confidence building course (think Peale's *"The Power of Positive Thinking"*). We rarely stop to consider that the issue might be a lack of self awareness.

Thorough understanding of self forms the base for so many things that make life full and worthwhile. We are happiest doing that which is aligned with our understanding of life's purpose, that which is in accord with our personal values, that which contributes to the process of becoming. All these things are possible only when we have done the work on self awareness and as we continue to deepen our understanding of self.

> **Thorough understanding of self forms the base for so many things that make life full and worthwhile.**

Personal Values

Personal values are an important route to self awareness and a good place to begin the search. A person's behaviour is affected in profound ways by their values, whether or not they are known. It is far better to understand our values as the basis of our actions than to wonder, after the fact, why we acted as we did.

Experience suggests that while life goals and vocation (what we are primarily responsible for) may change with age and family responsibilities, personal values remain consistent over a much longer period. Indeed, since articulating my own in 1995, I can now see that my values have formed the basis of my behaviour as far back as I can recall and that they continue to do so to this day.

ADDENDUM TO CHAPTER 1

Personal Values:

I worked on my values during my Durham time and in a three month fallow time the following winter. As introduced in Chapter 1 with further detail provided in Chapter 6, a value statement might be expressed initially in one or two words. It is important that this be fleshed out in a sentence or two and further explained in additional words.

As examples, I include two of my values and how these have been articulated from one or two words to a few sentences:

Personal Value in two words: UNITY and INTERDEPENDENCE.

Explanatory sentences:

"Humankind is but one part of the unity known as the universe, Creation, etc. Any action that affects one part of this unity affects all other parts in some way. The least part, the most insignificant element, is connected to the biggest, the most powerful. Interdependence is an irrefutable truth".

Additional explanation:

1. We will only be our best when all other parts of Creation are their best. We can only be whole when Creation is whole. Diversity is crucial.

2. Everything on earth is derived from and depends upon the earth for its existence.

3. When considering any action, we must consider its impact on all other parts of Creation. All parts deserve respect, care and service.

4. Solutions to life's problems come through community action. We are better together; we are nothing alone.

For my behaviour to be consistent with this value (and as my behaviour is a test of my commitment to the value) environmental concerns must always be front and center.

Personal Value in one word: INTEGRITY

Explanatory sentences:

"Security comes from integrity, from congruence of values and behaviour. The inner essence and the outer manifestation arise from the same source and must display congruence".

Additional explanation:

1. We must understand our personal values and live them consistently.

2. We can discover our essence, the core of our being, and there we will find our values.

This value requires that I always speak the truth and that my behaviour is absolutely consistent from one day to the next. My integrity requires that I seek the right action always.

CHAPTER 2:

Memories- Dungannon Doings, Part 1

Introduction

I've often told friends met after my early life in Dungannon that I'm related to everyone in Ashfield township. While this is stretching the truth a bit, it is only a small stretch. Scratching around beneath the surface relationships, you can usually come up with some connection, however tenuous it may be. Anyway, these are small stories story about some of my more notorious relatives and their adventures with misfortune and frivolity. Most of the stories are based on a fair measure of fact but I have taken some liberty in an attempt to nurture the myth of life in Ashfield township in the 1940s.

Grandpa and the outhouse

My grandfather on my dad's side was a fine old man by the time my memories started. He was born a few short months before Canada, in the same year. He gave over the family farm to my dad when I was still a babe in crib and he and grandma moved all the way to Dungannon, three miles away. He was 75 at the time and had just had his leg badly broken when he tried to single handedly stop one of the first cars in Lucknow. The car wasn't doing anything except driving down the street. I guess grandpa thought it was a runaway horse or something. Anyway, from that day forward, he walked with a cane and did not get around with much speed.

Grandpa spent lots of time on the farm during the day. Largely past working the farm, he spent much of his time under a big shade tree behind the house. Often, he would wander off to the garage, perhaps reminiscing over the many hours spent with machines, a large part of his working life. One day in the garage, he encountered a small black animal that looked at first like a cat. But it did not fool my grandpa. He motored out of that garage on a dead run, cane flying along with his old legs. "By jove," he said (his favorite expression under stress), "it's a skunk." We all retreated to his place under the tree to await the skunk who eventually strolled out, in its own time, unconcerned by the human turmoil it had caused. In all my time with grandpa, I never saw him move that fast again.

Halloween was a time of great fun for youngsters in my grandpa's time. 'Trick or treat' usually meant 'trick and treat' in those days. One of the favorite tricks was to turn over the outhouses that people used before indoor plumbing. My grandpa's toilet was one of those that annually got turned over. A family story has it that one year he ended up in a pile of human dung because the outhouse was not where it was supposed to be. In any event, grandpa came up with a sure fire way to keep his outhouse on its feet over Halloween night. The solution was simple. He would spend the night inside the toilet, on one of the seats (this was one of the modern 'two seaters'). Then he would be in a position to scare off those who would have his little house off its moorings. Somehow the perpetrators got wind of his plan. That night, they sneaked up behind the outhouse and tipped it over, on its door. Poor old grandpa was stuck inside, in a very uncomfortable position, until daybreak when grandma came to use the toilet and could not get in. From that night forward, he annually accepted that his outhouse would be upside down and had help lined up for the morning after to put it right.

What a wonderful old man, clever, ambitious, wise, gentle, forgiving. He would try almost anything and learn from mistakes. Toilets and skunks he knew not to fool with. I learned much from this old man.

Dad's big wagon

My father was a big man, the biggest of the five Stewart boys from the 4th concession. He worked hard with his hands and his arms throughout his life. In his prime on the farm, he was surely the strongest man on the concession and for some distance in every direction as well. During harvest, he would pitch an entire stook of sheaves onto the wagon, all the way to the top of the load. His feats of strength gave him some notoriety in the community. During the annual fall fairs, for example, the carneys would tighten up the bell wringer when they saw him coming. But he would ring the bell no matter how difficult they tried to make it. They eventually put a limit on how many teddy bears he could win.

Every year, dad would cut wood out of our bush for cooking and winter heat. Many years, he did the cutting alone, operating a two man cross cut saw by himself, a feat that very few men could do. When I was about ten, he took me back to the bush to help him with the cutting, one of the farm chores that I had not participated in to that point and that I was eager to learn. My job was to hold one end of the cross cut saw. That day, I learned how strong my father really was. I grabbed onto the saw, feeling quite grown up. Everything was going along fine until we cut into a tree, and then all hell seemed to break loose. "Have you got hold?" came from the other side of the tree. In response to my "yep", he gave a mighty pull on the saw and near pulled my arms out of their sockets. Then he pushed and the saw handles tore into my stomach. Before I could catch my breath, another pull. And another push. "Are you all right over there?" was met with silence which dad always took as a positive response. So more pulling and pushing and me holding on for dear life. At day's end, we had quite a pile of wood and a very sore body. Somehow I made it to the house (complaining was not in order). I slept well that night.

Dad made wagon racks in his spare time for other farmers. They would bring the wagon frame down and he would build them a rack. He was always good with big nails (he and I built a huge deck at our cottage in three days, when he was in his 70s). The rack would be finished in short order and ready for its intended purpose. Farmers often tried to outdo each other, partly, I expect, to relieve boredom and have some fun. Dad decided to build the biggest rack on the line for himself. So he set out to build the mother of wagon racks. And it was big all right. He finished just in time for the annual harvest and set out with his big wagon to the first farm to be threshed that year, about two miles up the concession. The other farmers who had gathered to help with the threshing marveled at dad's big wagon. "Sure is big, Mel" was a common reaction when he showed up. So off they set to gather the grain. On the first trip, dad had them load his big wagon to the gunnels. She came lumbering back to the threshing machine full of sheaves. On the way back, the load had to cross a shallow ditch that took excess rain water off the field. The front wheels made it over without mishap but the back ones did not. The load, unstable because of its huge size, tipped over and all the grain fell on the ground.

Nothing to do but reload it onto other wagons. They filled two and one half wagons with that one load from dad's big wagon. "Guess she was too big", they said and my father agreed. Anyway, the big wagon was soon only a memory in Ashfield township. Dad sold it to a farmer from the next county for he did not want to see that wagon again. From that day forward, dad's wagon racks were standard size.

Bachelor uncles and the foxes

My mother's dad died when she was only six. She had a younger brother, my uncle Bob. Suddenly, the household was without a male head. The position and its duties fell to two of mother's brothers, the oldest in the family. Uncle Gord was seventeen and his brother, Stuart, was one year his junior when they suddenly found themselves in charge of the farm. These two remained bachelors through their life, perhaps forever put off by the responsibility for six siblings and wanting none of their own children.

They tended the farm with good care and results, as attested by the fact that all eight of the children survived to ripe ages. As a child, I and my sister and our cousins looked forward to visiting with grandma and the uncles. They usually had time to show us the fishing hole and take us with them as they did the farm chores.

As the years unfolded on that farm, they would try out unusual things, perhaps to disrupt the boredom that can come with the routine of farm life.

And the way they became involved in these unusual vent[ ]
itself unusual. One particular venture involved raising fo[ ]
was working a field on contract for another farmer. At the
field, near the bush (all family farms had some bush in tho[ ]
a den of foxes. As the tractor continued round and round [ ]
nearby the den several times. Eventually, the mother fox decided her young
ones were in danger and she began to move them, taking each by the scruff
of the neck and hauling them off to safety. In the process, she dropped one.
In my uncle's words, "I jumped off the tractor and picked the little fellow up.
I took him home and fed him milk and bread. He turned out to be a she.
There was a fellow who raised foxes over in Blyth. We bought a pen from him
and had our fox bred to his male. Pretty soon we had a pen full of foxes".

Now what do you do with foxes after you have fed and housed them
through to maturity? Not many foxes were raised domestically but those that
were ended up as fur. My uncles became very fond of their foxes and would
have no part of sending them off to the fur factory. Some stayed with them
until a ripe old age. But at some point, I guess they just got tired of feeding
and housing their foxes.

On one of my visits, I helped my uncles open the pens and let the foxes
into the wild. We had to chase them to get them to leave. Obviously the foxes
had become fond of my uncles. We never knew exactly what happened to all
of those freed that day. But one huge black male, obviously not used to life
in the wild and maybe not liking it much, ran out in front of a truck and was
killed that very same day. The driver of the truck delivered the dead fox back
to my uncles.

From that point for several years, uncle Stuart would go into the bush in
search of his foxes, to see that they were alright. We went with him sometimes
but were not as adept as he at sneaking up without a sound. So most times,
he went alone.

Jean Reid and Honey Bill

Down the sideroad from my uncle's farm, just around the corner on the 6th
concession, lived another family of Reids. The matriarch of this family at the

e of my first memories was a determined woman of towering stature (in more ways than one) named Jean. She was strict with those around her but kind to kids who came visiting and in her later years, she would sit and reminisce for hours. Like many other older people, she had few visitors and little to do beyond minding the cats that hung round the old barn. She pined for the old days before the death of her husband, Honey Bill Reid.

Now you would think that with a name like Reid (mother's maiden name), we wouldn't have to scratch far to find a relationship. But this one was not so close. Turns out that Honey Bill's father and my mother's grandfather were brothers. So I guess that I was something like the fifth cousin, once removed, of Jean Reid.

Honey Bill got his name because he kept honey bees and produced honey. I was always intrigued by his name. I wonder now what Jean called him in those intimate moments when there were naught but the two of them (their union produced two sons). I can imagine her calling "come to bed, honey Honey".

We used to get our annual supply of honey from Honey Bill and his boys, and what wonderful honey it was. Much later, when our children were around, we would go to the honey place and Honey Bill's son, Jack (Honey Bill had passed away by that time) would show the kids how the honey was extracted from the honey combs and pour us out a pail of the freshly produced golden liquid that tasted so good. It was a special treat coming directly from the farm, one that we miss. We must remain forever grateful to farmers like Honey Bill from whom we learn that milk does not come from the corner store in plastic.

Uncle Gordon and the junk yard

Members of a family normally share a common personality, born through their genes, similar to that of their forebears. When the personalities of the parents, from whence siblings arise, is very different, the result will naturally be seen in differences in the children. Such was the case in my father's family. Grandmother Stewart always seemed to be serious. While not prone to fits of despair, she nonetheless maintained a stern disposition which suggested an intensity that made it difficult to smile even in the face of frivolity that left most others in stitches. This may have been due to her long term struggle with diabetes which required daily doses of insulin through a needle which she gave herself (enough to sour anyone's disposition). Grandma was devoted to her church, motivated by a sense of guilt common in those days.

My grandfather, on the other hand, always seemed to have a glint in his eye. He was able to see the fun in all things and took neither himself nor any situation encountered all that seriously. He went to church sometimes, usually to placate grandma who was out to save his soul along with those of the rest of us for whom she felt responsible. Grandma would tell stories of hellfire and damnation. Grandpa would relate his real life experiences in narrative form with funny twists that held our attention. You were always sure that grandma was telling what she saw as truth. With grandpa, you were never quite sure that there might be a bit of larceny afoot as he spun his tales.

I guess it was only natural that their children would pick up the personality traits of one or the other of these strong minded people. And so they did. Two of them, including my dad, were most often serious. Three were always laughing. And the last wanted to be funny but life's circumstances were unkind and so he ended up just confused, by nature unable to be serious and not having much in his life to laugh at.

My uncle Gordon was one of the funny ones, the uncle with whom I share not only my curly hair but also a wit that some hold is sharp and a low tolerance for boredom that keeps us hopping to a new place. But uncle Gord went places where even I dare not venture. He was at different times a farmer, a store keeper, an actor, an evangelist, a painter of barns and a member of the local Salvation Army band. At one time, he was training to be a missionary, but abandoned that cause to form his own church and a religion that had as adherents only he and a few friends and that, I expect, only he understood. His love of the demon gin often got in the way of his otherwise good intentions. As regular as clockwork, in the intervals between his devotional periods, he would resort to drinking with a passion. But he did most everything with a passion.

And he was forever laughing, at least during the many times where I crossed his path. His laugh was infectious though often misplaced. At my sister's wedding, uncle Gord showed up in an outlandish suit of many colours, having consumed more than a bit of gin. From where I was seated in a pew near the front, his laugh was quite evident. While aunt Ethel (who saw herself as God's gift to the temperance movement and worked away at her mission with unbridled energy) did her best to keep him quiet, he laughed his way through the entire ceremony. The poor minister, who did not know my family well, could not figure out what was going on, so he rumbled through the process as quickly as possible, very obviously thankful when it was over and he could get back to serious theology. My uncle was convinced that God could see the humour in every situation and so should he.

In the last several years of his life, uncle Gord lived in an old abandoned school bus that had ended up in a junk yard. This is the part of my uncle's story that I fondly relate to friends who did not know him. The bus had fortunately ended up on its wheels so did not list too badly. One end of the bus was taken up by a big double bed, jammed in with no space on the sides. Uncle Gord pressed his clothes by putting them under the mattress and sleeping on them. This was also a convenient place to store clothes that were not on his back, for closet space was at a minimum. At the other end, near the entrance to the bus, was a small propane stove that served to both heat the bus and cook his meals. There were a couple of chairs, old, stuffed and not uncomfortable. And a small cabinet that held foodstuffs, cereal and cans of soup. And of course at least one bottle of gin for cold days. When it got really cold, he would venture back to visit his long suffering wife and take up residence in her house until it warmed up. But he was not allowed any drink stronger than tea so left as soon as he could stand the temperature.

On one visit to uncle Gord's haven, he proudly explained that he had insulated the bus for the coming winter (the draft through rust spots on the bus made a fan superfluous). I asked him to show me how he had done that. Like all he did, the solution was simple yet effective. He had merely surrounded the bus with a roll of tin, about three feet high and then filled in behind this with sand. Having stilled the cold wind of winter storms in this way, uncle Gord spent most of that winter in his home in the junk yard.

Some thought he was crazy. Some didn't appreciate his apparent irresponsible attitude to life and the fact that he had survived so long without steady work. Some condemned his drinking and his lack of stability. Some held that he had abandoned his wife and family. But I loved the crazy old coot. He could spin a great yarn, tinged with truth and liberally sprinkled with fiction of his own making. He was the only one who could relate the family history. But most of all, I loved him for his laugh. And I regret not a bit when folks see something of uncle Gord in me.

ADDENDUM TO CHAPTER 2

The prime purpose of chapters that appear at first reading to be off topic is to encourage readers to do their own writing. Often memories can stimulate reflection as you ponder the question "what did I learn from this experience?"

A few things that I have learned from this chapter on memories:

1. From Grandpa and the outhouse: the wisdom gathered from a life of curiosity, good humour and paying attention. The obligation to pass it on in stories as I reach the age that grandpa was when I was a lad.

2. From dad's big wagon: the importance of trying, fixing and trying again. When something doesn't work out, move on.

3. From bachelor uncles and the foxes: one does not abandon a friend, even those with fur.

4. From Jean and Honey Bill: more memories from the farm including the source of sustenance.

5. From Uncle Gord and the junk yard: how to keep laughing through hardship and the value of a simple life.

I leave it to the reader to ponder further lessons from my stories and encourage you to write your own stories, using these ideas or whatever you can imagine that brings forth important life lessons.

CHAPTER 3:

Self Awareness, Personal Characteristics and Capacities

Inevitably, as the understanding of self deepens, life simply becomes better. Confidence and self-esteem are enhanced along with balance and a sense of inner peace. The self aware person has built a set of characteristics needed for the best life which also serve as the foundation for developing relationships and serving others in need of leadership.

> ## as the understanding of self deepens, life simply becomes better.

Sense of Purpose

The importance of meaning to human life fulfilled has too often been undervalued. People thrive when life has purpose and once again, self knowledge is critical. When one is fully aware of the self, purpose becomes apparent seemingly without additional effort.

Decisions on whether to take on a role become automatic as only those that fit the particular person's life purpose are guaranteed to produce a sense of fulfillment. Tasks which do not fit are then taken on with full realization that they may soon cause discontent. Boredom and lack of fit very often lead to failure; it is far better to leave the assignment to someone else for whom the task might be consistent with their life goals and sense of purpose.

Personal Feeling of Peace

In a new book, "*The Anatomy of Peace*", the authors point out that inner peace arises for an individual when we "honor the sense" that emerges naturally when we encounter a situation. If we meet a homeless person in need of a meal, our natural reaction is to help. Honoring the sense requires that we stop everything and help.

If we choose to "betray the sense" by acting against our natural inner desire to help, our heart is at war. We know the feeling, the sense of discomfort that emerges when our busy schedule demands that we simply walk by the homeless person without a word. We cannot escape the sense that doing so was in some way wrong.

A heart at peace leads to a sense of fulfillment, a healthy personal life, and a life able to contribute to a healthy community and world.

Self awareness comes into play once again. As we deepen awareness of self, our ability to choose the path that leads to inner peace grows and with it a storehouse of inner peace. Once we achieve a heart at peace, even for a short period, we want no more to be at war with our self. This feeling encourages an ever deepening search for self with the consequent positive outcomes on many dimensions.

Integrity

From the Taoist, we learn that integrity is evidenced by alignment between the inner essence and the outer manifestation. The fundamental prerequisite for a life of integrity is a thorough understanding of the inner essence, another way of thinking of self awareness.

Integrity is manifest when the behaviour of a person is absolutely predictable, when the leader reacts in a consistent manner so that others are able to predict, with a high degree of assurance, how the leader will react to a given set of conditions. Integrity also requires the ability to differentiate right from wrong and the motivation to choose the right path.

A person who is solidly self aware will exhibit integrity through actions consistent with his/her inner self.

Balance

A common complaint in modern life is "my life is out of balance; I'm spending too much time on x (often work) and have too little time for y (often family or fun)".

Balance is critical for a full, healthy life, a life capable of its full contribution as leader. Yet so many suffer from lack of balance, many working too long and hard, others with inadequate sense of purpose. So many of those who suffer in these ways fail to make the choice to seek balance; instead, they simply carry on with a life out of whack.

In so many cases, failure to understand self is at the root of the failure to seek balance, for balance is a choice that anyone can make. Through self awareness, a person will come to understand the vital nature of balance in maintaining health and purpose so as to be effective at dealing with whatever is the cause of lack of balance in the first place.

Transparency, Openness, Honesty, Authenticity

It is very much easier to live a life characterized by complete openness. The ability to be completely honest in all dealings with others makes for meaningful and effective relationships. Telling lies or hiding the truth in any way leads to lack of trust and can often have very negative results as evidenced by recent business failures and corporate and political leadership disasters.

Telling the full truth is the only way to be certain that your story does not change on the next telling (particularly true as your memory fades). As we make mistakes, we must be quick to admit to them, learn from them and move on. This is particularly the case in the social media context as several budding politicians have discovered to their dismay.

One cannot be authentic unless one first understands self and is willing to 'put one's self out there' for all to see, warts and all. Experience suggests that getting the skeletons out of the closet is a security measure for if they are all out there, no one can find a skeleton when the chips are down and something hidden can negate the good efforts of an entire life of otherwise sterling contribution.

> **One cannot be authentic unless one first understands self**

Self Confidence

Experience in coaching suggests that a sound understanding of self is foundational for self confidence. We will be confident of our ability to tackle the toughest assignment when we know our self and understand our capacities. We will be in a position to predict our reaction to issues that emerge along the way and equipped to deal with them.

Approaching a task with an honest understanding of our abilities will allow us to be realistic about the likely outcome and to seek out the help required without feeling inadequate. Success that results from our efforts, in concert with the required assistance, adds to self confidence and reinforces the importance of self awareness.

Humility

Arrogance is very often a manifestation of lack of self esteem. A person with low self esteem will often compensate by an outburst that has the appearance of arrogance (going 'over the top'). Self esteem (self confidence) is directly related to self awareness.

Humility, the characteristic on the opposite end of the scale from arrogance, is made possible with the self confidence that accompanies knowledge of self. I am confident and secure in self knowledge so that I have no need to display my confidence through an arrogant response to (whatever).

When encountering arrogance, the first question ought to be "can I help you become more aware of self and your reactions?" The second domain in emotional intelligence is self control, which is only possible from a base of self knowledge. Humility, one of the most highly valued of human characteristics, depends on self awareness.

> ## Awareness of self leads inexorably to humility.

Awareness of self leads inexorably to humility.

ADDENDUM TO CHAPTER 3

The following questions might seem obvious from the content but are offered to stimulate further reflection.

Sense of Purpose:

1. Does your current work give you a feeling of purpose?

2. Does your life have meaning? Are you making a contribution to your community? To the world?

3. Do you suffer from boredom in your workplace?

4. What do you plan to do about your current situation?

Personal Feeling of Peace:

1. Can you remember a time when you knew what you should do but did not do it? What was going on that caused you to avoid the right action (no time, other priorities, etc)?

2. How about a time when you stopped and did the act that you knew was right?

3. How did you feel after each experience?

Integrity:

1. Have you had a boss who would say yes one time, no the next, to the same question?

2. How did that make you feel?

3. What impact did that have on morale, yours and that of the team? On team performance?

Balance:

1. Do you give enough time to the many demands of you? Which suffer? Why?

Transparency et al:

1. Do you always speak the truth (to power)?

2. How do you feel when you speak truth? When you tell an untruth?

3. Do you communicate in an open and complete way? Why or why not?

Self Confidence:

1. Have you had a situation where you felt incapable? What was going on?

2. What contribution do you make when you are feeling fully competent and confident?

Humility:

1. How do you feel toward a person who acts arrogantly?

2. How do you rate yourself on an arrogant/humble continuum?

3. What reaction do you get from team members to your approach? Why?

CHAPTER 4:

Self Awareness, Relationships and the External World

As we deepen our understanding of self, a number of capacities develop that enhance relationships and make a significant contribution to our work, to those we lead, to our community and ultimately to the world.

Emotional Intelligence (EQ)

Daniel Goleman, the expert on the important concept of emotional intelligence, reports that success in life and leadership depends to a much greater extent on EQ than on IQ. His seminal work outlines and provides details on the EQ abilities categorized into five domains by Salovey. These domains, in the order in which they must be learned and applied, are: knowing one's emotions (self awareness); managing one's emotions; motivating oneself; recognizing emotions in others; and handling relationships.

The first of these, self awareness, is the foundation on which the other four depend. "This (self) awareness of emotions is the fundamental emotional competence on which others, such as emotional self control, (and understanding and inspiring others) build".

Empathy

Self awareness and EQ provide the base for an understanding of the needs of others. Consideration of the other and his/her needs is a necessary condition for an empathetic response to their needs. One cannot empathize with another in a situation of need without first understanding how they themselves might react in a similar situation. Here again, the importance of self awareness becomes evident.

Courage and Personal Security

Self awareness brings a sense of security, a feeling that I am safe in whatever situation I encounter ("I am different from and more than the situation; I will still be me when the current situation has passed").

Personal experience has provided a strong indication that when I am fully aware of self and willing to 'put it all out there', I achieve a powerful sense of security, knowing that there is nothing else to be discovered that can cause me harm.

when I am fully aware of self and willing to 'put it all out there', I achieve a powerful sense of security,

Think of those who put their name forth for political office only to be devastated by some disgraceful act in their past life which they had previously kept hidden from others and perhaps even from themselves. Far better to deepen the search for self, to understand self as fully as possible, and then to tell the world before it needs to know.

Courage comes with this sense of security. I can take risks from this position of security, content in the knowledge that nothing will shake my sense of self.

Gus Lee describes courage as the opposite of indifference. A person fully aware of self and the obligations that come with that cannot be indifferent to needs, whether they are for items basic to life or for leadership.

Courage arises from and is possible only with a deep understanding of self.

Trust

Trust is the basis of so much that makes life worthwhile and one's contribution all it can be. Those who are trusted are better for themselves and for those who trust. Trust is a characteristic that is so very highly valued by the best leaders, and for good reason. Nothing worthwhile results from a collective effort that is conducted in an atmosphere absent trust. Indeed, trust is the basis of teamwork; absent trust, a team will achieve little. Ergo, trust must be earned and preserved by all who would lead.

Perhaps obvious but nonetheless worth specific mention, the most profound level of trust can only be achieved by those who have a deep awareness of self and the willingness to be completely open and honest at all times. Lack of self knowledge can lead, almost without exception, to information important to best outcomes being hidden, often without intention (we are not aware of what we are hiding). Hidden information has a way of inevitably getting out, often at the worst time, with a consequent negative impact. Those who lack self awareness are unable to understand the potential impact, even if they are aware that something is indeed hidden.

Trust demands self awareness at the deepest level possible.

Change and Transformation

Leadership almost always involves change and frequently transformation (profound change). In many cases, the most urgent call to lead comes when an organization faces a difficulty from which transformation is the only way out.

Those who have successfully faced personal change are best equipped to help others do so. As in the process of becoming fully human, the base for success in personal change is self awareness. Those who are fully aware of self will proceed through the change willingly and will come out the other side with their heart, mind and soul intact.

During a period where I provided leadership to a significant change in corporate strategy, the team recognized that a corresponding shift in corporate culture was needed. This shift was accomplished by helping company staff through the personal change required for success in the new culture and strategy. The first step, you have already guessed, was getting everyone in touch with their self and building self knowledge.

Many who learn to lead have faced personal transformation (think of the MBA graduate, the successful manager, who realizes that management skills are not relevant in the current situation). Those who are able to negotiate through the trauma of personal transformation are then able to better help others do the same thing.

The starting point for success in personal transformation is self awareness.

Personal Destiny, Vocation

We are happiest when we feel a sense of purpose, when we feel fulfilled. In turn, we are fulfilled when we are pursuing our vocation, especially if we achieve a feeling that we are actually working toward our destiny, a lofty goal perhaps, but one most certainly worth striving for as evidenced by the feeling of those who believe they have discovered it.

The more we understand about our self, the more likely we are to be on a path to our destiny. There is simply no possibility that destiny can come to the fore absent self awareness. We simply cannot be sure of our calling until we are pretty certain of who we are (the answer to 'who am I' must precede an answer to 'what am I to do').

Many people come to the end of their working life, the period when their contribution has the greatest potential, with a feeling that they have wasted their time, that there was something of greater impact that they should have been doing. Experience and intuition point to a lack of self awareness as the root of this discontent. Those who spend time in their early life (at least early adulthood) on a search for self suffer no such fate. Time for reflection that might be otherwise used for action (what many 'hard nosed managers' consider 'soft, fuzzy' and a waste) proves to be time well spent.

(the answer to 'who am I' must precede an answer to 'what am I to do').

Pursuit of vocation toward fulfillment of destiny requires knowledge of self. There is simply no other way.

Decision Making Ability, Toughness When Needed

Once a person is fully aware of self and what drives their personal behavior, they are equipped to deal with whatever they encounter. Decisions come easily regardless of the severity of the situation.

In contrast to the loud, bombastic approach of those considered hard-nosed, the self aware person confronts difficult situations calmly, fully confident in their ability to deal with such. Self awareness enhances the capacity of the leader to be tough when that is required and to deal with difficulties in a timely and effective manner. Results of the actions of the self aware leader are almost always better.

The Capacity to Love

As self awareness grows, so too does the capacity to love. Along with courage, empathy and the other personal characteristics that hinge on self awareness, the capacity to love is critical to effective leadership. One cannot inspire others (a basic responsibility of the leader) absent a deep capacity to love those being led.

> **One cannot inspire others (a basic responsibility of the leader) absent a deep capacity to love those being led.**

ADDENDUM TO CHAPTER 4

Emotional Intelligence (EQ):

The five domains of EQ, according to Salovey (see Daniel Goleman's book), are : knowing one's emotions (self awareness); managing your emotions; motivating yourself; recognizing emotions in others; and handling relationships.

An exercise I have found useful is to rate yourself on each of the five domains. How do you rate on each? Consider why that is and what you must do to improve your capacity on that domain. For example, if your self awareness is good but you have difficulty controlling your emotions, you might improve by role playing with a friend who is prepared to challenge you.

Empathy:

So much of your capacity for this important capability depends on EQ. Remember that empathy requires that you go further than 'walking a mile in their shoes'. You must also really understand their context which will likely be quite different from your own.

Courage and Personal Security:

1. Have you backed away from a situation that promised conflict? For what reason?

2. Are there things about your personal background that you keep hidden? Why? Is there a risk that something might be found out that will limit your future career/life options? What do you intend to do to mitigate the risk?

3. Have you ever tested your physical capacity? Did that also test your courage? How did you feel when the experience was completed? What impact did that have on your ability to confront conflict in a work setting or a personal relationship?

Trust:

There are two approaches to the trust issue: you can trust all people until an individual is proven untrustworthy; or you can trust nobody until an individual proves they can be trusted. I have adopted the first approach and believe it is simply a better, happier way to live.

1. How do you approach trust? Does that affect other people's trust in you?

2. Have you trusted someone who has let you down? What was the impact, short and long term? On your relationships with the individual? On performance, yours and theirs?

3. Have you had team members who you could trust and others you could not? What was the impact on team performance of each?

4. Can you see the link of self awareness to trust? Your ability to trust others? Your personal trustworthiness?

Change and Transformation:

1. Have you been involved in an organizational change effort that did not work? Have you been able to determine why that was the case?

2. Does your workplace pay attention to or spend time thinking about organizational culture? What might you do to stimulate attention to culture?

3. Have you personally undergone a transformative experience? What did you learn about yourself as the change unfolded? How might you apply that learning to your workplace? To your life beyond work?

Personal Destiny, Vocation: (see Chapter 10)

Decision Making, Toughness:

1. How would you describe your boss? Where does she/he fit in the arrogant/humble continuum?

2. How does your boss deal with conflict? How quickly does she/he act to address and deal with it?

3. Can you relate the ability of your boss to make tough decisions to their arrogant/humble characteristic?

The Capacity to Love:

1. Have you experienced love in your workplace? How has that been made manifest?

2. How do you feel when someone shows love toward you?

3. What are the sources of inspiration for you (what inspires you)? What impact does this have on you (your ability to inspire others, performance at work, treatment of family)?

CHAPTER 5:

Memories of Dungannon, Part 2

Aunt Mattie's cookies

My grandmother Stewart began her life as Mary Ann Richardson. She had a brother, George, who was a wonderful old man when we first met. He had farmed in the hollow at Port Albert for many years. The road access to his scenic place on the nine mile river was a narrow gravel road that you did not use unless your destination was the Richardson farm. The main highway ran through Port Albert, bypassing my great uncle's farm. In the mid 40s, uncle George built a small house in the Port and retired. He wanted to watch the cars go by, having seen precious few during his life on the farm. Alas, in a few short years, the highway was rerouted to bypass Port Albert. The new road ran through the hollow right past uncle George's farm.

Uncle George was a bit of a carpenter. In those days, farmers had to be a bit of a lot of things, not really expert at anything but able to do most things with some level of proficiency. He was loved by all in the family so some gave him work or involved him in building, knowing his love of the trade, so long as someone was there to provide some supervision and help.

As he aged, he became a bit feeble but still wanted to help. I recall him helping build our first house in Goderich in 1956. My father was working in the city at the time. He would come home on the weekends and work away at the house, leaving uncle George with instructions during the week. On some occasions, uncle George would get finished with what he had been left to do and start on something that had not been discussed. Often when that happened, dad would spend the first part of his weekend tearing out and redoing uncle George's extras. One time in particular, my uncle had put in the beam to hold the bathtub. It was a big piece of wood that required several big nails to hold it secure. Uncle George did not spare the nails. All day Friday, he hammered six inch nails through this beam in a very awkward place in a small space. You guessed it. The beam was in the wrong place. It took dad all morning on Saturday to pull those nails out. As mom would have said, "the air was blue" that Saturday morning.

Uncle George married Martha Green, a local girl, and they settled down for a life on the farm. Aunt Mattie was a scary old thing. In her small retirement home in the Port, she kept everything in its place and would not tolerate any disruption of her ordered life. My sister, Mae, and I would live in some terror throughout every visit. We would be warned ahead of time to "sit still, don't touch anything, don't say a word". We sure looked forward to a few hours of that once a month. But as much as we were frightened of aunt Mattie, we loved uncle George and if we could get him out of the house, we'd have a good time.

Aunt Mattie must have had a heart in there somewhere for she made good cookies. Every time we visited, she would bring out the cookies. We were never sure how many to take, fearing that she was testing us to see whether we would succumb to temptation, for she was a preachy type of person as well. We would take one and give her our best cute little kid look. If it worked, she would invite us to take another. But after two or three, the cookie box would disappear. "You wouldn't want to be too good to the kids for fear they might come to expect that you loved them" seemed to be her attitude. Perhaps that is why her son rarely showed up to visit his father and mother.

But aunt Mattie sure made good cookies.

Mary Rivett and the heavy muffins

Dungannon had a wonderful bake shop in the 40s and 50s. Eedy's had been baking bread and sweet things for years, serving the village and surrounding farm community as far as Auburn. Every day, the Eedy's truck rolled out of Dungannon, loaded with fresh bread, donuts and tarts, bound for customers whose tongues were hanging in anticipation. The arrival of the Eedy's truck twice each week was something that we kids surely awaited with eager anticipation.

My first job off the farm was at the bakery. Shortly after my thirteenth birthday, Irvine Eedy asked if I could help out on Saturdays when the demand was high and help was needed. He offered to pay me $3 per day which was big money in those days. So off I went every Saturday morning about 5am to the bakeshop. My task was to help Isabel, an Eedy by marriage to Ross who ran the family farm. Her specialty was tarts, pies, donuts and muffins. So at an early age, I became a maker of tarts and other sweet things, a skill that I would often call upon in my later teen years when I discovered girls.

Mary Rivett, who delivered the rural mail, would come to the bakeshop every Saturday to buy a dozen muffins. There was no mail delivery on Saturday so I guess Mary and her husband Tommy had time for a muffin with their coffee on the weekend, even though the story around the village was that they rarely talked to each other. In any event, one Saturday in the spring of 1955, Isabel called in sick. The other bakers were busy with their regular Saturday chores, baking bread and buns for the hungry crowds who would later descend on the store and for deliveries. It fell to me to make the muffins. I had seen Isabel make these many times so experienced no hesitation at the task. I assembled the ingredients, mixed them up and popped them in the oven.

In the prescribed time, I extracted what appeared to be a fine batch of muffins. We packaged them up and set them on the shelf to await Mary and others. In she came like clockwork to get her weekly supply and off she went to enjoy one while still hot from the oven. Well, no more than fifteen minutes later, Mary is seen marching down the street toward the bakeshop, huffing and puffing, with a box that looks suspiciously like a muffin container under her arm. In she stomps and demands that we take back these foul items and return her money. You bet. Something had gone wrong in the making. These muffins were so hard and so heavy you could break up rocks with them. No good even for basketball, for they wouldn't bounce.

That day, I discovered how you get out of doing something: simple, you just screw up. I was never again asked to make the muffins. Whenever Isabel was sick, we simply told folks there were no muffins today. And our customers were reduced by one in any event, for Mary Rivett never again bought muffins from the bake shop. One bite from one heavy muffin was enough to do her forever.

Bus Anderson and his unusual old model T Ford

No one remembers how Clayton Anderson got his nickname. He just was always called Buster, later shortened to Bus. The stories of his many escapades in the early 50s are legendary in the Dungannon area.

Bus was born the son of Jarvis Anderson and his wife Gertie. Jarvis and Gertie had three children, Bus and two girls, Verna, who later married Punch Culbert, and Millie. Some time later, Jarvis died, leaving Gertie a young widow. She in turn married Tom Parks, brother of Dick Parks. Dick's wife, Maggie, was a sister of my grandfather and their children were first cousins of my mother. One of the offspring of Dick and Maggie married my uncle Art, so my third cousin became my aunt Mary.

But back to Bus Anderson. Bus volunteered at the start of the second world war and while still a teenager, was off to Europe in the army. Oldtimers say that the army taught Bus how to drink. Wherever he learned, he sure learned good. Bus returned from the war with Cynthia, an English war bride and a fine woman, in tow. Bus seemed to the locals to almost always be in a drunken stupor but somehow he and Cynthia managed to produce six young Andersons.

Bus had an old model T Ford car that he drove around the back roads of Ashfield township. He bought the model T instead of the more fashionable model A for two key reasons: first because it was cheap and second because the T was virtually indestructible. Both reasons were important to Bus, the first because he never had much money and the second because of his penchant for driving into ditches and through fields, as often off the road as on it. Most often, he was too drunk to walk so he drove, a normal reaction at the time.

Many people have stories to tell about meeting up with Bus coming the other way, or helping him out of the ditch. My sister and her boyfriend, later to become her husband, were off to meet the uncles (apparently for their approval of the betrothal) when they met Bus coming down the sideroad. As usual, he was weaving from side to side, taking up the whole road. Dave pulled off the road and waited for the inevitable crash. Somehow Bus steered the old car to the left just enough to miss them. He slowed as he passed, rolled the window down, and shouted "I bet you thought I was going to hit you". And off down the road, laughing to himself in his perpetual state of bliss.

My favourite Bus story revolves around his response when he had hit the ditch for the nth time and was being helped out by some local farmer. On this particular occasion, he came barreling down the Dungannon hill. Just before the bridge, he hit a giant pot hole which propelled him and the T into the ditch. The old car gave a great heave and rolled onto its side. Those who came upon the scene say both Bus and the T were lucky they didn't end up in the river. But Bus was not dismayed for this was not his first time in the ditch. He's reported to have said, "I'm going to put wheels all round the old car. Then whichever side ends up on the bottom, I can just put her in gear and drive away". He thanked the farmer for getting the T back on the road, chuckled to himself, and was off in search of his next drink.

Incorrigible, considered of little use to family or community, nonetheless Bus made a big contribution to the local colour and became a legend in his own time. Alas, his affliction did him in at an early age, leaving poor Cynthia alone to raise the Anderson brood. Many of the local women figured she was blessed to be rid of Bus. Whatever she felt, she raised her kids well under very difficult circumstances.

Tommy Carmen Anderson

About two miles out of Dungannon on the Lucknow road lived Tommy Carmen Anderson. He worked a small farm more or less successfully as was the normal outcome for farmers in those days.

I knew little of Tommy Carmen and he remains mostly a mystery. Nor can I find any relationship to my family no matter how far or hard I dig. But I love that name. Tommy Carmen Anderson.

Alvin Sherwood is another one for whom no relationship can be found. He must have moved into the village from beyond the township boundaries at some point, for any native of Dungannon must surely have been related in some fashion. Alvin ran the school bus. I normally made it all the way home from high school but Alvin would truck no lapse in discipline and I spent more than a few nights at my cousin's place, having been put off the bus for some form of unruly behaviour.

Alvin had the word 'Dungannon' painted on the side of his big bus, for a reason that no one could ever understand. We used to kid our city friends that the bus was the village and that the village kept moving around the country. That was just one metaphor for how small the village really was.

As Forrest Gump might say, "that's all that needs to be said about Tommy and Alvin", so that's all that will be said.

ADDENDUM TO CHAPTER 5

1. Aunt Mattie's Cookies: there is good in everyone, sometimes in the cookies.

2. Mary Rivett: a life lesson that I have tried to remember (sometimes we stretch our capacity too far) and one that I try to avoid (screw up to get out of work).

3. Bus Anderson: the perils of addiction and the importance of laughter.

4. Tommy Carmen Anderson: sometimes it takes very little to amuse me (and that is alright).

With the foregoing as background on the critical nature of self awareness as foundational for life and leadership, we now turn to several ways to initiate the search for self and to contribute to a growing understanding. In other words, it is time to address the question "how do I discover who I am?"

In order to remain faithful to the promise of reasonably short bits that can be read and considered before boredom sets in, many of the suggestions requiring more detailed description begin on a new page. Some of these are best pursued on your own, through introspection and private reflection. Others require the help of a friend or mentor for best results. Off we go then.

CHAPTER 6:

The Many Routes to Self Awareness

A precondition of creativity is a mind empty of the distractions, busyness and chaos of our 'normal' existence (Taoism, paraphrased liberally).

The search for self awareness is one that needs conditions similar to those required for the creative process. Ideally, one should come to the process free of distractions, able to concentrate on the important task. We know the contribution that focus makes for ordinary tasks. We finish tasks more easily, quickly and with better results when our attention is directed to the task in the absence of distractions (how often have we said, or thought, "don't bother me with that issue until I am finished with this one?").

It should come as no surprise that the same logic applies to the critical task of enhanced awareness of self. The more we can distance our self from our normal situation, the better able we are to dig into what makes us tick. Active minds that have difficulty with deep reflective practices can often find a route through 'abnormal' distractions, putting a new frame in the mind, something completely different that in a sense distracts from the distraction. By thinking about their reaction to the new frame, people learn something about their self. Repeating the process deepens the understanding.

Since the search for self is very likely completely different from your day to day work, the work you do to discover self should take a completely different route. At the end of the day, reflection is critical to the process, the deeper the better. The more complete the change of venue and situation, the farther from normal, the better.

Personal experience suggests the following as ways to both initiate and deepen self awareness; all of these are approaches that have worked for me and for those whom I have coached.

The Search for Personal Values

Personal values are foundational to self awareness because of the impact of one's values on their behavior. Whatever approach is taken to enhancing self awareness must be directed toward understanding your values at the most fundamental level possible.

I have used a number of approaches when asked to help someone identify their personal values based on my experience in fleshing out my own. These often begin with a simple question and proceed through more complex questions and other processes as the understanding evolves and deepens. Many people see little value in self awareness and must be convinced that time spent on gaining an understanding of self is worthwhile. This can be done using the arguments in chapters 3 and 4; eventually one of these will resonate and the search can begin.

The question that I (as coach or facilitator) begin with is designed to get at what the person holds as foundational beliefs. Asking them to complete the sentence "I believe ..." is a simple and non-threatening way to initiate the process. Many times it is necessary to stimulate the response by offering suggestions of how the sentence could be answered. Sometimes other simple questions help (for example, "what do you consider important?"). Initial responses to the completion of the sentence often provide clues that can be explored further. For example, if someone offers "I believe in the importance of family", the coach might ask the respondent to explain, or ask "what is it about your family that is so important to you?" The role of the coach in all cases is to take whatever opportunities arise to deepen the enquiry.

As the seeker becomes increasingly engaged in the process, presenting them with a list of possible values and asking them to choose the most important has proven effective. Presenting values such as courage, ambition, humility, and family forces the respondent to select those most important. I use a list of about thirty possible values, ask that they select their top five or six and then prioritize those by allocating a percentage to each. In this way, personal values are both selected and prioritized so that a decision can be made when forced to choose between conflicting values.

The seeker can be presented with a number of pairs of values and asked to choose. This is a way of narrowing down a list and deepening understanding.

For example, if the seeker is having difficulty with the choice of five priorities and comes back with more, the coach can stack each value in a pair with all the others and ask them to choose. In that way, priorities are derived. My experience suggests that a list of five to ten values is best (I have identified ten of my own).

Since personal values always affect behavior, another way to derive those values is to reflect on how one has behaved in situations that call forth values. For example, if one always runs away from any hint of conflict, it is clear that courage cannot be a value; it is likely that safety or security is more highly valued. If one always gives priority to work in spite of family needs, then work and associated values (could be ambition, wealth or something else) are clearly more important than family.

A further step is to ask the seeker to describe a situation that confirms each of the priority values. I once helped a young man who avowed that family was his most important value and a couple of visits to his home confirmed to me that he was sincere and correct in establishing this as priority. In a conversation at the same time, he told me that he could not afford the costs of his household as he was working in a community support role that paid him less than a living wage. While the role he was in was consistent with another of his values, 'care for nature', this second value was of a lower priority than family. This was causing him considerable personal stress, as is always the case when values and behavior are out of sync. As we discussed his situation, the lack of alignment between his priority value and his behavior became evident. My advice, which he subsequently followed, was to seek a job with the pay scale that he required. If family is the value to which you ascribe highest priority, you must provide for their needs above all else.

Once a list of values has been developed, it is important that the values be fleshed out so that the implications of each value are clear. For example, if 'courage' is a priority value, one might develop a phrase such as "when in a situation of significant conflict, I will always have the courage to do the right thing". If the value is 'family', the phrase might read "if my work conflicts with the needs of my family, the latter will always be given priority". This additional step allows the individual to periodically check their behavior against the values derived and reflect on any deviation, thereby deepening self awareness each time the values/behavior check is done. In my case, these checks are done annually and my level of comfort with the values and value-statements increases every time consistency is confirmed.

The importance of a deep understanding of personal values cannot be overstated. A young student that I coached explained during a coaching session that she had a set of values for her work life and a different set for her time away from work. She was in a difficult working environment with a supervisor who was described as 'awful' and felt that the different values were necessary to support her personal sanity. I have encountered similar attitudes from many people over the years. When I explained to my student that personal values truly understood do not change to accommodate different situations, that you take personal values with you to all circumstances, and helped her to flesh out what was really important to her, she gained a measure of comfort and contentment that she had not previously felt. This helped her to understand why she felt stress in the work situation and that the issue was the responsibility of her supervisor. With this knowledge, she was better able to cope in the current situation and ultimately changed her occupation to work that was a better fit with her personal values.

If we have understood our personal values correctly, we can be assured that our behavior will always conform.

A Completely Foreign Space

For those able to do so, the preferred approach to deepening a sense of self is to get completely away from it all, into a space that is foreign to one's home location and normal experience. This can be thought of as a type of sabbatical. To make headway on self awareness, one must venture out alone, absent family and friends, to avoid taking distractions along. Support of partner and family is critical as a precursor to the process.

Often one can find fellowships and other mechanisms that help with cost if time can be allocated in the midst of busy lives. The effort required to identify support and decide on location is always worthwhile.

> **one must venture out alone, absent family and friends, to avoid taking distractions along.**

I have been able to get away several times over a span of twenty years. In each case, I ventured forth with some sense of a goal but lacking complete clarity of the likely result. This lack of clarity allowed creativity to enter and made the result better than could have been imagined had I tried to nail down the details before hand. In a sense, one must go forth with faith that the result will prove the effort to have been worthwhile.

Each of my times away were initiated for somewhat different personal reasons but always because of a felt need for a break from current reality, usually after a period of intense work pressure and a feeling that my contribution to the particular work was declining and the need for my presence was at an end. I embarked each time with a sense that I was being called to something different that could not be defined in the midst of the pressure of the work. As one seeks vocation, self awareness is bound to accompany what is discovered.

A month in Durham, England served as my first foreign space. A friend referred me to the principal at the Church of England's St John's College attached to the University of Durham, one of three British universities with a college system (the others are Cambridge and Oxford). I explained that I wanted to study and reflect on life for a month and while admitting this to be an unusual request, he agreed to entertain me. In the event, I was given room and board and access to a tutor and to any courses underway, all for the cost of maintenance, a whopping 14 British pounds per week.

I recall another friend with whom I discussed my plan to ask for a reading list ahead of time suggesting that I "just go and see what transpires", sound advice which I eventually followed.

For this experience, I had a clear goal of discerning vocation. Not having a guideline for such, I began by designing a detailed process with nine steps and then working through the process (see chapter 11), a clear indication of my need for structure at this point in my search for self awareness.

The process unfolded through a series of questions, beginning with "why bother, for this will take effort and both the process and the outcome may prove to be uncomfortable?" and including a detailed account of my life history. Writing a story of my life proved of significant benefit as I reflected particularly on what was going on when my life's trajectory changed. What, I wondered, were the factors that influenced the shift and what did they suggest about me?

I returned from Durham with clarity on vocation at that time. The Durham experience gave me a good start on my personal values which I fleshed out in greater detail during the following winter, having left the work in which I had been engaged and in the fallow time before embarking on the new role.

A few years later during another fallow time between community roles, I went back to school full time for a school year. I was in the midst of study toward a degree in philosophy and moved for the year to a university in another city with my spouse this time. Studying full time in class with students much younger proved to be a most fruitful learning experience about the subject and myself. My comfort with the subject was an indication of the importance of the philosophical approach to life and further proof of what I had learned about myself through prior experiences.

In the early part of the new century, I accepted an invitation to teach a course in environmental issues in Uganda. While the development and delivery of the course required hard work and long hours, giving little time for reflection, I came from Uganda with new understandings of self. Volunteering for this sort of work in a setting so different from normal is bound to have an impact as it had for me.

Another few years and one more pressure-filled community role had me yearning for another break. This time, a friend pointed me to a fellowship at a divinity school in the eastern U.S. I applied for and was awarded the fellowship which covered room and board and tuition for a school term during which I studied theology with students in the final years of schooling leading to ordination in the American Episcopal church. During this period, most of which I was on my own, messages kept coming at me about vocation and approach, further deepening my sense of self.

The flexibility created by limited expectations proved the Taoist correct; when the mind is cleared of distractions, creativity takes over.

In each of these get-away times, I came to the experience with a fairly clear sense of what I would be doing for the entire period and as a result, the outcome was reasonably close to what I had expected, although the sense of calling that emerged from my Durham time was completely unexpected. In each case, except in Uganda, I had time for reflection with limited distractions beyond the need to attend class and complete the assignments. Thinking about this now, the expectations with which I arrived at each experience limited the flexibility that could have led to greater understanding.

A couple of years ago, I embarked on the fourth of these experiences absent any sense of what I was doing, what I might encounter, or clarity on goal or expectations. I had good reports from friends who had pursued the experience but I admit to some trepidation about going alone. Having made travel arrangements, I set off in autumn time to walk five hundred kilometers on the pilgrimage to Santiago de Compostela in northern Spain. This was to be a time of deep reflection and complete flexibility. Each day (twenty-one in my case) the pilgrim, on his/her own as was I, walks and thinks. There is little else that one can do but think. The flexibility created by limited expectations proved the Taoist correct; when the mind is cleared of distractions, creativity takes over. The clarity that results is a thing of great wonder, simply amazing.

Getting into a foreign space is a perfect way to clear one's mind so the important work on self awareness can be done. It is better if one can go alone to limit the distractions that attend with partner, family or friends. My experience suggests that goals established ahead of time should be limited to allow whatever will emerge to become apparent. There is no better way to create space for deep reflection than to find a space that is remote and unfamiliar. If you are fortunate enough to have a supportive partner and a secure relationship, go forth alone and find yourself.

Recreational/ Physical Pursuits

Time for and attention to reflection often accompanies recreational pursuits, some of which seem to call forth more learning than others. One such pursuit that has worked for me is hiking in the mountains of western Canada.

I have completed the West Coast Trail twice and in both instances, the experience of the trail proved of profound significance as a test of my capacities and as a contribution to self awareness.

Mountain experiences are most often times when reflection seems almost automatic as one ponders the meaning of life in relation to the wonder of nature. One can think of such questions as "how much value do I place on nature?", "what is the limit of my physical capacity and am I enjoying this?" and "how significant is my life and contribution in the context of planet earth?" In all cases, it is important to reflect on the meaning derived from these periods of reflection as a contribution to increased self awareness ("what is this saying about who I am?").

Recently, I embarked on another process of discovery, this time on the East Coast Trail. I undertook this experience on my own, with little knowledge of what I might encounter, since the information available was skimpy and no one could be found who had hiked the trail. Planning for the trip, I considered this a test of courage and physical capacity, uncertain about weather and trail conditions. Arriving with complete flexibility and no particular expectations, the eleven day hike along the trail proved yet again the power of walking and thinking on a trail with, in this case, magnificent views of the Atlantic.

Self awareness is bound to grow in the midst of the majesty of the mountains and the mighty sea and from the physical effort required.

Educational Pursuits

Life-long learning is critical to success in life and in leadership. Self aware-ness grows along with pursuit of additional learning at any stage of life. My experience suggests that study of subjects remote from those studied for the purpose of career add most to self understanding, the greater the distance between the areas of study, the better.

In my case, engineering and business were studied for job purposes. Additional areas of study included political science, religious studies, phi-losophy and theology. As the nature of educational pursuits broadened, each additional discipline added to awareness of self and, incidentally, enhanced my capacity on the job.

Pursuit of additional learning while also working ensures that the student encounters a very different situation after the work day is over. In my case, I encountered a feeling similar to that of being in a foreign space, although not quite so significant. As learning of these new subjects grew and I became more aware of my feelings toward the content of the learning, the connection to my personal values became more apparent. I found a subject with which I was more comfortable than I had been with my first areas of study. I discovered that I related more closely with philosophy than I ever had with engineering.

Literature on Leadership

Perusing the leadership shelves in book stores, with a focus on new books and unusual approaches to the subject, can provide a test of your understanding and reinforcement of what you have learned. Because of the interest in the subject and the impact that has on book sales, new books appear frequently. I visit a local book seller every two months and quite often pick up a new book. A few years ago, I found Gus Lee's *"Courage"* at a time when a group I was coaching had asked for a session on the subject. While the book stayed on the shelves only for a short time (I conclude that sales fell short of initial projections), the content of the book, particularly a chapter of core values, proved to be of significance.

Of course, it is not only new books that prove helpful. You will find support in older literature such as the work of Machiavelli, the biographies of Churchill and the spiritual/ religious texts of ancient times. I am also certain that you can find books in the Self-Help and psychology sections of your bookstore but my focus has been on leadership lessons.

If you are working with a friend, coach or mentor, sharing what you have learned from a given book can save you time and energy, for there are any number of books written on the topic that are of limited value. One of the benefits our group coaching process added for participants was our recommendations on what they should read and avoid.

What are others saying and reporting

Often others see things in your behavior that are indicative of who you are. Just as often, others will hesitate to report anything that they consider negative or to which they think you might react negatively (they may have had experience with you that strongly suggests you do not want negative feedback).

Kouzes and Posner ("A *Leader's Legacy*") point to the importance of a 'loving critic', a friend who sincerely cares but is also willing to criticize when that is warranted and needed. What we have most often instead is either an 'uncritical lover' or an 'unloving critic', neither of which helps us to become more self aware. The first serves only to maintain our current state and the latter can become so annoying that we simply disregard their criticisms. I have had the good fortune to have a friend who questions everything, my loving critic.

It is important that you develop relationships with others that encourage them to provide feedback when they encounter things in your behavior that help you gain awareness of self. The value of loving critics to our personal growth is significant. By facing the impact of your behavior on others, your emotional intelligence will grow along with awareness.

Sometimes you may receive feedback in written form. This can prove to be of even greater significance since people are more careful when asked to record their thoughts of another person. Written comments provide both an opportunity and an obligation to reflect on their meaning and the contribution they make to self awareness.

While perhaps less important as you age (you have less time to adjust), the comments should be encouraged and welcomed at all times. Recently, I received a written comment from a student evaluation process that I had made an inappropriate comment to a female student. While I cannot remember making the comment, this was further evidence of a rather cavalier attitude to verbal comments that I consider humorous while recognizing that others do not share my sense of humor.

Journals, Blogs, Articles and Books

As the last question in coaching sessions, whether with a group or a single individual, I always ask "what have you learned about yourself during this session?" I explain the justification for the question by stating that this is the most important question for those devoted to the deepest understanding of self. Getting into the habit of asking this question of yourself in every situation is a certain route to gaining self awareness.

Another habit that is of significant value is writing down your responses to this important question. Writing brings additional clarity and depth to the thoughts on which your answer is based. As you think about what you have learned in words that you will want to record, the learning takes on added meaning and more focus is brought to your awareness of self.

Journaling is a good way to initiate the recording process. As you begin, your journal can be a very simple record of whatever you consider valuable enough to retain, a few words to remind you of what seemed important at the time. I try to carry a simple journal with me and any thoughts that seem of value in the absence of the journal, I make a note in my paper calendar, later transcribed in my journal. I locate each comment with a date and a record of with whom I was meeting when the thought came to mind; also included are any actions that I have agreed to undertake.

I check my notes periodically to identify themes and trends in my thinking and to consolidate what I have learned about self. Further, I have a record for the next meeting with the same person to maximize the value of our ongoing conversation. An example of an entry in my journal is a quote from a friend- "I would rather feed someone than meditate"- the single entry from an hour of conversation.

Once the discipline of journaling is firmly established, a blog should be considered as a contribution to others' learning but also as a means of deepening your own. This increases the formality and clarity required for your note must be in form and words that are understandable to others. As you construct what you will include in your blog, you must reflect on how you can make something you have learned of interest and value to another person. This has the effect of increasing your personal self awareness as you ponder what you would want to know if someone else was writing the blog.

Individual blog postings can be a few words or a few paragraphs but should never be longer than the time your intended reader can maintain interest. Learn from the pastor who admitted that he wrote a long sermon because he did not have time to write a short one. In framing a blog and putting flesh on the frame, your words must be clear and your content limited. Take time to reflect and write the short, crisp and clear sermon.

I developed a blog site specifically for my pilgrimage to Santiago, my first venture in the blog-o-sphere. While not certain before the pilgrimage began that I would have content deserving of a record, in the event, I recorded over fifty posts during the twenty-one days of walking.

Writing articles on issues that stir your passion is another way to enhance learning of self. You might experience, as have I, these as longer versions and further exploration of the themes that emerge in your blog posts. Once you get comfortable with your articles, find a way to get them into the public sphere. I write a regular column in our parish newsletter and each column reinforces my level of interest in a community issue. Periodically, I send articles to the local newspaper for consideration and have had several printed over a period of years. By reflection after the article has been printed and receiving feedback from readers, my interest in the issue is translated into further understanding of my personal values and my awareness of who I am.

> **Take time to reflect and write the short, crisp and clear sermon.**

A final approach in this area is to take what you have learned about self and life in general and put it into book form, ideally ready for publishing. This formalizes your learning further and each word, paragraph and chapter is an opportunity to reflect on the awareness that has grown with each of the experiences you describe in the book.

I have written and self published three such books and the themes have evolved with the experiences that surround the times of writing, from my first book on citizenship. Each has been deeply personal, including what I have learned from my many experiences as well as how I was affected by each and how I felt as I encountered new and unusual situations. The middle book was entitled simply *"Things I Know"* and was intensely personal.

As a contribution to self awareness, if you have the patience required to write and stick with it through the publishing process (which need not be long if you follow the self-publishing route), self awareness will grow in significant ways that cannot be replicated by any of the other writing/recording techniques.

Verbal Story Telling

Each time we tell the "who am I" story, we learn something more about our self. Verbal story telling is an art form that, having lost favour over many decades, is now increasingly recognized as having value in any number of settings. Story telling is a critical skill in the creative process since ideas that cannot be communicated effectively end up on the dust heap, never seeing light beyond the gleam in the inventor's eye. At the same time, there is precious little in our education system, formal schooling and beyond, that is designed to develop the skill.

Recently, working with a team of community story tellers, I led the development of a story telling course targeted at nonprofit sector leaders. In the delivery of the subject, the students were required to develop and deliver verbally a "who am I" story. In the event, we proved our assumption that by telling such a story, the students discovered things about themselves of which they were previously unaware and often admitted to things that they had never before verbalized.

Learning to tell stories, focusing initially on telling one's own story, is a route to self awareness at the same time as the capacity to 'tell and sell' is enhanced. As we tell our stories and enhance our capacity to do so, the contribution to our leadership capability is huge.

Mentor/Coach

Engaged in a discussion on the definition of mentor several years ago, it occurred to me that the essence of a mentor was captured in the phrase "a wise old friend". As the conversation continued, we added "someone who is always available to contribute what he/she has and you need". Taken together, these two phrases described what the two of us felt was important in a mentoring relationship.

Many people who seek a mentor seem to want nothing more than advice on how to advance their career. Often when looking for a mentor, these folks look to the person to whom they report or to someone at a higher level in the organization. To my mind, that is career counseling and, while important, it does little to contribute to self awareness, which should always be the goal of a mentoring relationship.

In coaching someone on identifying a mentor, I suggest seeking someone who is as far removed as possible from what the seeker is involved in at present. My reasoning is that you learn less from the familiar than from the remote and that by exploring new areas, you often discover something about your likes, needs and wants that you would never notice while playing in the familiar sandbox. People are nervous about asking another to be their mentor. My advice is to just ask as most people are honoured to be considered and rarely turn down a request. Often too, a mentoring relationship will develop organically from initial conversations on family (or even the weather) to a closer and deeper conversation over time.

A successful mentoring relationship is one where the mentor does not let their protégé off the hook. The 'why' question must be front and center (some advocate asking the question four or five times). If the goal is deepened awareness of self, as it should be, the conversations must go deep. My coaching partner, in his book *"The Mentor's Mentor"*, has a series of questions that move the conversation ever-deeper, all directed at the goal.

Protégés can also learn about themselves by listening and learning from the life of the mentor. The person whom I consider my most important mentor, Dr Grant MacEwan, lived a full life with many career twists. I learned from simply listening during our many conversations, from his books and from talking to his other friends.

Similar learning is also possible through a coaching relationship. The difference is that a mentor most often contributes his/her time and wisdom voluntarily while a coaching relationship is more formal and the coach expects to be compensated. My experience suggests that mentoring is most often more satisfying and effective and easier to try/assess/fix. If a mentoring relationship is not working, it is easy to disengage whereas once a coach has been contracted and money has changed hands, the protégé is reluctant to end an unsuccessful run because of the investment.

Whichever approach is taken, having another person to evaluate your learning to a given point and to point you to the next deeper step is always a good thing.

Thought Experiments

"When you start to consider your legacy, you begin to live life as if you matter" (Kouzes and Posner, "A Leader's Legacy").

In my coaching practice, a number of exercises have helped people reflect on what is critically important to them and how they can determine their life's purpose and, through that understanding, achieve a life of contentment and happiness. These 'thought experiments' are initiated through a limited number of focused questions.

The first questions build on the quote from Kouzes and Posner. Simply asking "what legacy do you want to leave?" stimulates reflection on the long term goals of the individual and the gap from their present circumstance. This can be expanded by a more detailed thought experiment. I ask those who seek help to consider the future when they will have retired after a long career. Their co-workers and friends have gathered to say farewell and many have agreed to say a few words. "What are they saying about you?" is the question. "What would you want them to be saying?" is the unstated implication of the question.

A more personal approach is to ask the student to write their epitaph. "What would you want written on your gravestone?" is the way that I phrase the question. As examples, I share my response to the question, admitting that it has changed with time but has been stable for a considerable period. My initial response, several years ago, was "he was a decent man". This evolved through "he tried to help" to that with which I have been comfortable for an extended period right up to the present in the words "he never started dying", indicating that I intend to keep learning/growing until my last breath.

Each of these approaches opens up the possibility to deepen the discussion and the understanding of self. In all cases, the response can lead to one or more 'why' queries by the coach that encourages added reflection during the coaching session and beyond. For example, the initial response to the legacy question might suggest a limited long range goal that does little to test the capacity of the respondent and makes only a small contribution to community. The coach has a responsibility to point out the limited nature of the goal and encourage the student to dig deeper and think bigger.

While the questions might appear almost offensive at first, experience in using this approach has led to positive outcomes in every case.

ADDENDUM TO CHAPTER 6

Personal Values (a coaching approach):

As a coach, I proceed initially through a series of questions, the same questions that I used as I developed my own values. The sequence goes something like this:

1. Complete the sentence "I believe…".

2. If that does not initiate a fairly quick response, ask "What is very important to you?"

3. For each response, ask "What is it about that value that makes it important?"

4. When a list of values has been identified, ask "Which hill would you be prepared to die on?" This is one way to identify priorities.

As the protégé is increasingly engaged in the process, present a list of values. I use 25-30, including the following: ambition; community; courage; family; happiness; integrity; meaning; nature; service; and wealth. Ask the protégé to select 5-6 of the values as most important. Then ask them to allocate 100 points among the chosen values with a higher number indicating higher value, more importance.

Another way of assigning priority is to put the chosen values into pairs and ask the protégé to choose the more important value. For example, you might pair happiness and nature. Choice of nature would indicate a strong environmental value, where the person was willing to sacrifice happiness to preserve nature.

When satisfied that the values have been identified properly, help the protégé flesh out a few sentences that clarify each value and to think about what each means in terms of self awareness. The question "What have you learned about yourself from this exercise?" should remain in the forefront.

A Foreign Space:

My experience suggests that some structure is almost always helpful to get the most out of time away. The work of David Lonsdale or my more formal structure might be of help, although the latter can limit creativity if followed to the letter. Some questions to stimulate creative thinking on your ability to get away:

1. What is it about your current work that limits your ability to get away? What will happen if you are not in place for a month?

2. If you were awarded a sabbatical, where would you want to go and what would you want to do (remember that a sabbatical is not simply a vacation)?

3. Where might you find help (financial, coaching, accommodation, etc) to follow your dream?

4. What actions, taken now, would assist in a time away in say two years?

Recreational/Physical Pursuits:

1. How often do you hike the mountains or sit on the seashore?

2. What do you do to test your physical capacity?

3. What do you have on your bucket list in this area?

4. What is restricting your ability to get at bucket list items?

Educational Pursuits:

1. What have you always wanted to understand?

2. Think about educational pursuits that are as far from your learning to date as possible. Are any of these on your list from question 1?

3. What resources are available close at hand to fill in your learning blanks?

4. What would you have to give up so that you could pursue night courses? How important are those things?

5. Does your workplace have programs to support further education?

6. What does further study do for your future prospects?

Literature on Leadership:

1. What are you reading right now?

2. What was the last book you read on leadership? When?

3. What is the next book that you plan to read?

4. Do you have a friend with whom you can share a reading list?

What Others are Saying:

1. Think about your reaction to criticism including that offered out of love. What do you think your reaction evokes from the person who has offered the criticism?

2. Do you have a friend who will serve as loving critic? How close is the friendship?

3. What do you talk about when you get together with him/her?

4. How do you think they will react if you ask for honest feedback? Will they invite you to do the same?

Journals, et al:

1. Do you maintain a journal? If not, why not? If yes, what do you record?

2. When you face an important question or a difficult situation, do you make a record of the question, the context, the answer, the action taken?

3. Have you ever written a blog? If so, what did you blog about? What was the reaction of friends and others who have read your blog? Were you inspired or discouraged by the reaction?

4. Do you read blogs from other people? If so, what do you get out of them?

5. Do you ever get upset enough to write a letter to a newspaper editor? Have you followed through? If not, why not? Was your letter printed? How did you feel whether it was printed or not? Are you inspired to write again?

6. Where would you go for help if you wanted to write and publish a book?

Verbal Story Telling:

1. Is there a tradition of story telling in your family? Who is the story teller?

2. Are you comfortable in telling stories verbally? If not, why not?

3. Do you find yourself telling stories at work to sell your ideas?

4. How might you learn to tell stories and practice the craft? Do you have a friend with whom you could share stories?

Mentor/Coach:

1. Do you have a mentor? If so, how was the relationship formed? How long have you known the person? How well do they know you?

2. What is your relationship to your mentor (work, family, friend, school mate, etc)?

3. How often do you meet? What do you talk about? Is the conversation helpful in advancing your awareness of self?

Thought Experiments:

1. What legacy do you want to leave? When your work is done, what would you hope to have accomplished?

2. What will have been your most important contribution to community?

3. Project yourself into the future as you retire. What are your friends and co-workers saying about you? What would you want them to be saying?

4. Your partner is placing a memorial stone over your final resting place. What words are going on the stone? What would you hope would be on the stone?

CHAPTER 7:

Blogs from Spain (some of fifty-one blog posts during the pilgrimage)

Dreams must never die (evening of day 2 of 21)

Last evening, I passed an aging priest. He was short and stocky, might have been Bishop Fred's brother. He looked sad and forlorn, all alone in the midst of the hustle and bustle of the square filled with the people of Burgos experiencing the joy of good companions.

> **Surely the period between the birth of a dream of great things and its death is the time when we are living life 'as if we matter'.**

When, I wondered, had he encountered his dream of changing the world, a dream that would have enlivened his soul and enhanced his contribution to his parishoners and community and his value to the world? (For his sake, I hoped that he had done so in his younger years).

And when did the dream die?

Surely the period between the birth of a dream of great things and its death is the time when we are living life 'as if we matter'. Just as surely, that is when we are fully human. For when the dream dies, our soul and our spirit must surely suffer and die along with it.

And if we are living in a way that we don't matter, what's the point.

Reflections on a Sunday afternoon (day 5)

The pace picks up.. and then it slows. Nothing like a few days of walking to quicken one's pace. Day 4, I made 6 kilometers the first hour and almost 9.5 in 1 hour and 25 minutes. That was at the start of the day.

Funny how the importance of making good time dissipates as the sun gets higher and the day gets warmer. By day's end, I was back to doing about 4.5 kilometers per hour.

Mellow must be part of the pilgrimage process. Again today, my mind seems to have gone completely blank. Tried to conjure up deep thoughts and none would come. The pilgrimage appears to have eliminated all sorts of things that normally preoccupy my mind. I assume that I am not alone, that others experience the same thing.

Eastern religions teach that to be creative, we must eliminate thoughts, clear our mind (different from the west where we assume the more things we can jam in, the better). Perhaps this is what is underway, the first step in a creative process. Would it be so.

And the churches, the magnificent churches. In days gone by, thoughtful people with great imagination and big dreams built the most wonderful buildings that continue to serve, many times as mere echoes of grander times. One cannot but be inspired by the architecture of those times. Walking into a church, one is immediately struck by the lofty ideals of former times and inspired by the magnificence of the high arches and striking altar pieces.

Both yesterday and today, buildings were built with a purpose in mind. Yesterday's inspire, today's facilitate (built today to be 'good enough'). Hard not to long for times gone by periodically, and never more so than when I enter one of these great churches, built so long ago.

What does God want of me (and you)? (day 6)

Evening of day 2, talking about religion to Jaap from Luxembourg, I said I read the Bible periodically for the life lessons it contained.

(NOTE that all biblical references come from the Mind and Memory of Wayne, version 2012, so forgive me differences from the version you use).

(NOTE also that I am not in the proselytizing business. I believe that everyone has the right to decide independently on a religion or on none at all; the following are comments based on the decisions that I have made).

Back to the topic at hand.

One of the Bible bits that has always held appeal is from Micah. To the question, "what does God want of you?" Micah gets the message "to act justly, to love mercy and to walk humbly with your God".

Clearly we are called to justice, mercy and humility, and I have long got that.

On the road on day 2, I was contemplating (not much else to do, maybe that was what called me here). It occurred to me that there are three other words in the direction that may be of equal importance. Those words are "act, love and walk".

Just as we are called to justice, mercy and humility, we are also called to act (what you do to the least), to love (on these two laws) and to walk (with those we serve).

These themes echo throughout the Bible. The inspiration on el camino clarified the intent of the lesson in a way that had not hit me before.

Not quite a 'Paul on the road to Damascus' moment but meaningful just the same.

The call is ever more clear... And the dream of a better world and my role in that is coming into focus.

My Pilgrimage Begins (day 7)

My sense is that my pilgrimage really started yesterday, a day of significant learning that continued today. I seem to have emerged from the mellow state into whatever comes next. And el camino has done it all by herself. I'm certain that this is part of the process that many must encounter over here.

I have taken to asking people why they are here, what brought them to the pilgrimage. Surprisingly, very few are able to articulate a response. Most give non-spiritual replies. Some just like long walks; one woman said "I had nothing better to do" (I hope she finds good stuff here).

Many young people report being between jobs or simply out of work. Some are seeking answers to what they should be doing ("I don't like what I am doing"). And then a few brave souls admit they are here seeking answers to the "what's it all about" question and with those I have had great conversations.

Me? I say that I am looking for what is next for me. It may be time for me to give up the big dream of changing the whole world and focus on individuals or small groups that I can really help through some particular difficulty. I think of Martha's work with a young immigrant woman and her daughter.

Borrowing from Bentham, if I can help one person escape the bonds of poverty, the world will be a better place, overall. Perhaps it is the big dream that I am to shed. I am confident that answers will come and that el camino will do her job. We'll see.

Thoughts during a sleepless night (day 12)

Rey Carr and I meet for a coffee and tea almost every time I am in Victoria. Coach, mentor, author, facilitator, all round good guy, Rey always raises questions that cause deeper exploration of one´s person and their soul.

So it was with his comment on my blogging. He posed a series of questions but the one that struck me as most insightful and thought provoking was "are dog biscuits [I brought a bunch to feed angry dogs and found no such animals] a metaphor for the person you were prior to El Camino?"

Last night, in bed with only my thoughts, I rephrased his question to "are dog biscuits a metaphor for what you must shed on the pilgrimage?" Made me think of what I must leave behind along with the dog biscuits.

Migod what that question meant for a night when I had hoped to get some sleep for it raised a whole bunch of other questions. I am still carrying about 2 of the 3 pounds of dog biscuits I came with. Why can I not just give them up? Are they a metaphor for the penance that I am doing, without realizing it? When will I shed them along with the bits of plastic that have lessened my load only marginally? Will I know why I am here when I am finally able to shed the last of the biscuits?

Made for an interesting conversation with myself during the night.

We are beginning to understand the power of myth (in the most important sense, as truth leading to understanding and wisdom) and metaphor (lessons relevant to our current place, time and situation) as, for example, a way of reading holy scripture. I am a fan of that process. So, why not when applied to one's life? What do we carry that serves as metaphor for something deeper?

I think of a bunch of stuff that I carry that limits my contribution. At this point, I do not know which of those I must and will shed but the process of discovery has begun. One of those may be the inability to walk at any pace but my own (back to Micah and "act, love, walk", I will walk with you so long as you walk at my speed; my tendency is to put action first).

I have spent a few days in a state of mellow contemplation, trying to think but thoughts have been elusive. That period, I believe, is now over, stimulated by Rey's question.

Hopefully, the creative process of 'what's next' will begin now in earnest. (Of course one of the things I must shed is over thinking everything).

We will see. Later...

Down and Up (day 15)

Are they opposites or are they an integrated part of the whole?

Been thinking of paradoxes and what we consider opposites all day as I walk up and down on el camino. I have long been fascinated by paradox. I encounter paradox all the time and try to learn from both sides of opposites.

Those who have hiked with me know how much I dislike going down any time before we reach the top of whatever mountain we are hiking. I want to maintain the height gain and do not like to go down only to have to come back up.

As I pondered that today, I realized that this might be another manifestation of my 'control freak' nature, maintaining control of gains in the hope they can be sustained.

But life is never one long upward climb.

We have learned that opposites are teachers. But for the opposite of any

It is pretty hard to go up from any-where but down. concept, we would not know the concept itself very well. Think, for example, of good and evil. Just maybe evil exists so we will know when we encounter the good. How about success and failure? I recall in the private sector that mistakes were given so little tolerance that people hid them. You cannot learn from what is kept under the overturned milk pail.

Years ago, I coached a kids' ball team. We had a mixed record until the playoffs when we beat the first place team even though down by three runs in the last inning. I was asked "how did your kids win?" to which I replied "because I taught them to lose".

So as I thought about down and up, it became apparent that they are really two halves of a whole, both part of the process of learning and growing.

It is pretty hard to go up from anywhere but down.

Another lesson from el camino where the towns we go through are almost always in a valley to which we go down and then we walk back up. A lesson we experience in every-day life and will learn from if we just pay attention. A lesson made much more vivid for me today.

Today's Question (day 17)

Can I maintain utility while toning down (perhaps denying) the characteristics that have to date made me useful?

The Final Question (day 20)

She did it again. I have lost any sense of control over here as el camino keeps taking over.

Tonight I went along to Saint Eulalia parish church in Arca, as much to put in time before bed as for any other reason. On the way in, I picked up a bulletin written in English announcing that this is the home church of Saint

Louis Guanella whose descendants carry on the tradition of devotion to the poor under the theme 'Bread and the Lord'.

Here is the question that was printed on the back of the bulletin: "Have you ever thought of spending your life for God and the poor?"

Reminds me of the African American priest in Cambridge who issued the challenge "If you ain't stepping out, you ain't got faith", a challenge that affected me deeply at the time.

So now I know what I was meant to shed and what I was still to carry.

Nothing is easy on el camino and nothing is difficult. One just has to pay attention.

[Note: you can find my entire 51 blog entries from Spain
at www.waynestewarttalks.wordpress.com].

ADDENDUM TO CHAPTER 7

Learning from 21 days on the pilgrimage was significant. While testing my physical capacity, the opportunity to reflect on the meaning of life and my particular place in the human family was of greatest value. Among the lessons:

1. The unity of humankind, reinforcing my personal value statement on unity.

2. The impact of a pilgrimage of this sort on an understanding of self.

3. The importance of a mellow period to clear the mind for the creative work that follows.

4. Many insights, such as the connection of up and down, which added to the store of wisdom, important to my role as mentor and coach.

5. An understanding of the role that control has played in my life, reflection on the impact of that on those around me, and a huge step forward in my ability to give it up.

CHAPTER 8:

The Special Case of Spirituality as a Disciplined Approach to Self Discovery

"This is work and that is religion and that has no place in this". How often do we hear this sentiment in our work place? Equally often, in my experience, we hear "this is religion and that is work and that has no place in this" in our place of worship. Both statements express an attitude that limits the good that can be brought from one discipline into the other. And yet, if we are to be authentic, whole human persons, doing our best in all circumstances, surely we have to be the same person in each place. Surely we must learn from all situations and apply what we have learned whenever the learning is called upon.

A degree in Religious Studies enhanced my understanding of comparative religious systems and their contribution to understanding of self. However, I am a practicing Christian and my learning from long practice in the Christian spiritual tradition and process has naturally had the most significant influence on the role of spirituality in my search for self awareness.

Most will agree on the importance of spirit in the workplace. We enjoy working in a place full of spirit and many of us will reject one that lacks it. We enjoy being around people who exhibit enthusiasm, who have an obvious and open sense of purpose, who are comfortable with self and others, who are oriented to caring and giving, who exhibit inner peacefulness. When the spirit in our workplace erodes, employee morale is not far behind. "It's not fun anymore" is a common lament in such circumstances. In cases where the spirit falters severely and cannot be recovered, the enterprise simply fails, dying along with spirit.

And yet many shy away from conversations that include spirituality. I recall teaching leadership to graduating MBA students, intending to introduce the value of messages from religious systems and having to use Taoism because, as expected, lessons from the dominant religious systems were rejected outright by the students. The role of the institutional place of religious practice (church, synagogue, temple, mosque) in turning people from this search for self is unfortunate. Bad experiences with religion in early life have caused many to shy away from anything that suggests spiritual practice, perhaps fearful that this might draw them back into a practice that they have happily rejected.

all religious systems offer a route to enhanced self awareness.

This is all so very unfortunate. As I have deepened my search while coincidentally pursuing Christian spiritual processes, I have come to believe that we can only discover our true self at the level of spirit. In Christian terms, the Holy Spirit, the legacy benefit left for the human race, resides within each of us. My sense is that my search for a deep understanding of self and my seeking of the Holy Spirit within is one and the same search. Finding one, I will find both.

As a further example of the contribution that can be made from close attention to the value of religious practice, consider that all religious systems offer a route to enhanced self awareness. The Buddhists seek nirvana through a staged process with each stage leading to increasing levels of self discovery. The Taoist approach to following the 'way' can also be seen as a path to greater levels of awareness of self and the spiritual writings in the Tao te Ching can be used as coaching tools in this pursuit (see John Heider's "*The Tao of Leadership*").

Finally, consider that many of the leaders that we hold up as heroes have had an obvious connection to spiritual practice. Martin Luther King Jr, Nelson Mandela and Mahatma Gandhi come to mind from the last century. Dr Grant MacEwan, well known to western Canadians, had a profound level of spirituality and was always willing to entertain a conversation of the subject.

We admire these folks and understand the importance of spirituality in their life and leadership. Surely we must learn from their experience and follow their path as a particularly relevant approach for the end is so important. Let us never again reject the spiritual approach.

ADDENDUM TO CHAPTER 8

1. Have you encountered the contention that religion and work must be kept apart? If so, what has been your reaction?

2. Do you know of people who have a regular religious practice? How do you think this has affected their attitude to others? Do they have characteristics that are appealing? Not so much?

3. Do you attend your place of religious practice regularly? Why or why not?

4. Have you experienced a spiritual workplace? Have you worked in a place where the spirit has eroded? What was the impact and how did you feel about that?

5. Are you aware of lessons from a broad range of spiritual practices? Do you think there is any value in broadening your understanding? If so, what do you plan to do?

CHAPTER 9:

Makes You (and me) Think

For several years, I wrote an article in our parish newsletter that was issued 3-4 times each year. Following are samples, once again as examples to encourage you to do the same. These display the contribution of a spiritual approach to enhanced self awareness. You may also identify the evolution of my thought over time.

An early article, from 2006

At our first contemplative prayer service on May 28 of this year, Rev MacLeod introduced us to a reading from the gospel of Thomas. The words that stuck with me were "only when you have come to know your true self will you be fully known- realizing at last that you are a child of the Living One".

In other words, until we know our self at the most fundamental level, we simply cannot be truly known by anyone else. Only when we find the Spirit within will we be fully human. Makes you ponder the importance of the spiritual quest.

Made me think of the many, many current books on the topic of leadership. The book stores are full of theories on what it takes to lead, most of them written for the business world. Whether one is a fan of Collins or prefers Secretan or any of a host of other experts on the subject, the common thread is the central role of self awareness.

The foundation for all leadership practice, indeed for confidence and competence in any endeavour, is a full knowledge of one's self. Humility, a characteristic receiving high praise from many current theorists, is based on self knowledge. In order to lead with boldness and humility, we must first know who we are.

It makes me think that this search for self is where the secular world and the religious world come to the same place. Surely the search for self and the spiritual journey are one and the same process.

Christians know that God created us in His image. He sent His Son to show the way and the Holy Spirit to sustain us. Surely, it is incumbent upon all to embark upon a serious spiritual search, to engage with others on a path to full understanding of this, one of the greatest of God's gifts, the indwelling Spirit.

One of the great benefits of the spiritual journey is that once we discover the Spirit, we will then know what role we are specially equipped to play in service to God's people and His Creation.

Makes you think that the role of the church may just be even more important than ever before, to people with a regular church practice and to those with none. It follows that our role must be to invite others to join us on this journey.

Whoo boy, lots of things make you think, eh?

From October, 2010, just after the civic election in which I was a candidate for mayor

This article will be a bit of this and a bit of that, reflecting my confused state a few days after the civic election.

Anna gave me a wee book, "Perseverance", by Margaret Wheatley, just after the election (a message for anyone who might be tempted to relax after a hectic period with no apparent outcome).

In an early chapter, Margaret says "this is how the world changes. Everyday people not waiting for someone else to fix things or come to their rescue, but simply stepping forward, figuring out how to make things better". She concludes the chapter with "now it's our turn".

'Stepping out' is a recurring theme for me. In my little book, "Things I Know", I write "failure to step out is a failure of vocation. We will not fulfill our obligation to serve until we step out".

Time and again, the message comes that one must step out from whatever is a place of comfort. To follow the call of Jesus requires that we step out in service to all in need, very often into a place of discomfort, a place in which we feel less secure (think "what would Jesus do?").

During the civic campaign, I often felt like Peter must have when he stepped into the sea. As his faith faltered, he began to sink. So long as his faith was strong, he was safe. So it must be with us as we step out in faith, confident that, in the end, all will be well.

One of the questions that have made me think at the end of a hectic period is "what did you learn about yourself from this experience" (see the lack of coherence of this article).

My immediate reply was "at my age, I think I have learned all there is to know". However, the question has made me think. If we remain attentive to learning at all times, surely we must discover something that we do not yet know of our self.

Lots of things make us think. Are we stepping out, following the admonition in Micah to "act justly and to love mercy and to walk humbly with our God?"

Where might we find opportunities to practice 'stepping out'? And what can we learn from each of the experiences that result?

Oh my tired head, all these thinks!

From July, 2009

Reading Barbara Brown Taylor's "An Altar in the World" has me thinking about the many things we do that provide an opportunity for spiritual practice and development.

Chapter 5, "the Practice of Getting Lost," is of particular interest as I encounter yet another period of my life where I am uncertain of which direction my life should take.

As one born on a farm, I was particularly struck with her invitation into the wilderness, for "once you leave the cow path, the unpredictable territory is full of life". She suggests that we "stop fighting the prospect of getting lost and engage in it as a spiritual practice instead".

Made me think of the times in my life when I have felt most fully alive, times when I had embarked on a new adventure, uncertain of the path let alone the destination. Often it seemed that I became more aware of God in those situations (perhaps my need for security simply made me more attentive to the presence of God). Made me wonder if that is what Brown Taylor had in mind, if I may have been on a spiritual journey without realizing it.

Made me think of the eastern tradition of the third stage of life, the 'forest dweller' stage, where practitioners enter the 'forest' to reflect on life and their calling from here forward. And what about Jesus' time in the desert as he prepared for an active ministry and more?

Barbara Brown Taylor calls us away from the narrow path on which most of us spend our life, the path worn by our "frugal, fearful hooves". If we never learn from the experience of being lost in modest ways, we'll have a most frightful time when confronted with a really big loss.

Perhaps that is what divides our church, I thought, as we struggle to reconcile conflicting theological opinions. Could it be that those who have never experienced "the holy art of being lost" are holding tight? On the other hand, could those comfortable with loss initiate change for the simple sake of a new experience?

Sure had me thinking and that likely achieved the author's purpose. Getting lost as a spiritual practice? A time when life is full, when the spirit soars. What could be more spiritual than that?

Made me think of the silent prayer I say each Sunday when we are called to a few moments of silence. "God, help me know the way" is a prayer for the safety of the narrow path. Perhaps what I should be asking is "God, help me get lost", confident that in the wilderness, I will discover God, my spirit and my life.

From May 2011

I was introduced to Bluegrass music in the film "Oh Brother, Where Art Thou?" and have enjoyed it ever since.

One of the songs in the movie begins with "Oh death, won't you pass me over for another year?", a plea that many people make when faced with the possible end of life. We have learned to fear death and go to extraordinary measures to avoid it, even as quality of life gives way to pain and drudgery.

Thinking of this in the past month as my mother approached the end of her life. Wise and determined to the end, she had left explicit instructions to "do nothing extraordinary" to maintain life beyond her time. She knew that there would be a "time to go" and she would be ready. And she was.

This year's Lenten series, an exploration of the work of Marcia Faulk, gave comfort and got me thinking at the same time. The last session was of particular help as it focused on "Sustaining Life, Embracing Death". The short poem, "Leaves," reminds us that "Leaves don't fall. They descend". And "In their time, they'll come again".

Surely that is the message of Easter. As Marcia points out "death is not a destination: it too is a journey to beginnings: all death leads to life again".

We celebrated mother's life at a service on Easter Saturday, between Jesus' crucifixion and resurrection, perhaps particularly appropriate for a woman whose life and her attitude at the end was a model for the rest of us. As with all who are important to us, mother lives on in our memories and the stories we tell. The reflections of her grandchildren as we celebrated her life provided confirmation.

Lessons from a Jewish poet/liturgist and a Christian mother add to the many from the life, death and resurrection of our Lord, Jesus. As we face life *and* death with wisdom, dignity and hope, we serve those we care about in the best possible way.

An Easter season that will have me thinking for some time.

ADDENDUM TO CHAPTER 9

These few articles provide further evidence of the insights and understanding of self that arise as one writes for publication, however small the audience reached by the words.

CHAPTER 10:

Vocation: Good Work

"I urge you to live a life worthy of the calling you have received."
(Paul's Letter to the Ephesians 4:1)

In *"The Reinvention of Work"*, Matthew Fox says that we must differentiate between good work and bad work and then only take on the good stuff. In his formulation, good work is sacred work that engages our entire being including our soul. Good work is that which is consonant with our core values, that which builds upon our self awareness and allows us to maintain our integrity at the highest level. Good work alleviates the stress and inner conflict suffered when persons are engaged in work that does not accord with their personal values, Fox's bad work.

As we proceed on the path to self awareness and deepen our understanding of personal values and self, questions about our life's good work will emerge. "Am I doing the right work? Could I be doing more? What should I be doing? Is there something out there that only I am suited to do?" These and similar questions will enter our thoughts and demand a response.

Often when we are in the midst of a career change, we are helped along by someone who helps us answer the question "what do we really like to do?" We should resist the temptation to believe this helps define our vocation (calling) for there is a big difference between

there is a big difference between what we like to do and what we should be doing.

what we like to do and what we should be doing. Simply doing what we like to do is not sacred work and eventually will lead to the same sense of disquiet from which all bad work suffers. Following our calling is doing what we should be doing, our good work.

For most people, particularly those with families, priorities shift with age and family responsibilities. As such, good work may take on different meanings at different stages of life. At any stage, however, work must always contain meaning and be attuned to personal values. If the values of the organization for which you are working are in conflict with your personal values, you have a choice to suffer through this or to find another organization with a value fit.

A lesson from the Hindu religion is instructive, although focused solely on men. After family obligations are fulfilled through paid work, the man enters the 'forest dweller' stage where he actually leaves his family and goes off into the forest to contemplate life and discover the way forward. Beyond this stage, which can take several years, he returns to society in the 'sage' stage and offers the wisdom he has gained to others, as teacher, mentor, guide. He has found his good work and a life worthy of the calling he has received.

At some point in each human life, the thought of calling will arise, at least for certain for those who pursue a path to self awareness. In my view, the sooner these questions arise, the better. We may not be in a position to enact what we discover, for reasons of other priorities and obligations, but understanding what we should be doing and looking forward to a time when that is possible can add meaning in an otherwise dreary situation devoid of our good work.

How then can we discover what we are called to be and to do?

Christians have become familiar with the concept through the life of the saints, many of whom have received the call in a flash of light, a sudden inspiration, a dream or some similar experience. Paul on the road to Damascus is the most vivid example. Yet not many mere mortals will receive the call in this manner. We must labor to discover it or labor on without it, often in a life devoid of meaning, inspiration and potential. The discovery of a call produces a comforting outcome, bringing peace and good work. The result is worth the labor and the pain of the journey.

The best, happiest life, the life in which we are all we can possibly be, the one in which we make the biggest impact, is possible only when we discover who we really are and begin to practice that, in other words, when we are engaged in our personal good work.

There are several ways to approach discernment- the process of discovering a calling. Some people may wish to follow a structured approach as in my Durham experience. Others advocate simply being open to opportunities as they arise. The latter approach requires that one has the flexibility needed to dive in, often only possible when you have earned a pension that allows regular periods between roles for which you are paid, times when no added income is needed.

I have benefited from both approaches. In the unstructured approach, I have been recruited into two senior level roles in the nonprofit sector by a friend who knew of my passion and capacity for the work and of my availability to accept the job. This approach requires that you stay in touch with friends and keep them alert to your situation, as I did by reporting that I was "not busy enough".

Now turning to a structured approach...

Addendum to Chapter 10

1. When you consider a career change, do you ask yourself "What should I be doing?" If so, how do you go about finding an answer to the question?

2. Have you experienced a time when you had to take on a role in which you did not find meaning in order to support your family? How did you feel during that period? Are you still in the role even if your needs have changed? If so, what are you going to do about that?

3. Are the values of your organization consistent with your personal values? If not, what are the key gaps? How serious are the gaps? What impact does this have on your integrity (do you find yourself defending the indefensible)?

4. Are you always able to do the right thing in your daily work?

5. What have you done to determine your good work? Do you have a friend who knows you well enough to steer you to the role that is just right for you? What can you do to develop such a friendship?

CHAPTER 11:

Discernment in Durham

I have long been fascinated by people who abandon the mainstream to 'follow their call'. When queried on the subject, they are almost always unable to answer the 'how did you know' question. As I embarked for a month-long personal retreat at a Church of England college in Durham, England several years ago, I was determined to explore the subject and had high hopes of actually identifying my good work.

The only literature that I could find on the process of discernment was in a little book by David Lonsdale ("*Listening to the Music of the Spirit*") targeted at the religious seeker. His four step approach- prayer, information gathering on options, analysis and decision seemed similar to the 'what do you like doing' approach and was not likely, I thought, to lead to a satisfactory outcome.

Lonsdale's work did encourage me to try a structured approach and on arrival in Durham, my first task was to develop the structure. As I developed and then worked through these nine steps, I was often aware of a presence, from a source that I could not readily identify, and finally had to admit to the possibility of divine intervention coming most often at just the right time. The outcome of this discernment approach was powerful and profound, so right for me.

In anticipation and hope that this process might provide the same outcome for others, helping them discover a sense of call in the midst of the craziness of today's world, the steps in my discernment process are presented below. Writing what is learned at each step moves the process along and allows checking back to ensure logical consistency and coherence.

Step 1: Why Bother?

Discernment can be a tedious and painful process and the result can be disturbing and a lot of added work for it will invariably involve change. Thus, the process must be undertaken for good reason.

For me, the answer had two facets: first my duty to pursue my calling/destiny given the urgency of the times, and second, my growing dissatisfaction with the current work situation. The initial stages of a sense of boredom had set in. I have come to believe that boredom was a clear signal that I was being called somewhere else.

> **boredom was a clear signal that I was being called somewhere else.**

My current role had provided meaning for some time but my sense was that I had made my contribution and I had lost a sense of purpose in the role. A need for renewal was evident, for both me and the organization, and the effort to complete the discernment process was justified.

I wrote at this step: "*My age and energy both pass with time. I can no longer say 'yes, but tomorrow', with any certainty that I will ever get to it*". This is indicative of a clear sense of urgency so off we go to the remaining steps.

Step 2: My Life Story.

Looking at critical events in one's life helps bring focus to two critical questions: "who am I" and "what do I bring to the table (material and personal resources)". This was important background for an objective analysis of my being, my strengths and my preparedness. Not surprisingly, this is also an important step in the search for self awareness for integration of self and life role is vital for reasons given in other parts of the book.

It is particularly important to focus attention on turning points to determine what was going on and where each might be pointing. This focus on turning points, from childhood to the present, limits the review and makes it manageable, given the importance that it be complete.

I wrote at this step: "*I learned that I could help others discover and fulfill their destiny while neglecting my own*", further indication of the importance of the task before me.

Step 3: Material Possessions (My Having).

Prior to proceeding further, I looked at what I have, the material possessions accumulated over time. This step was taken to determine what my needs and those of my family were and whether these needs block or restrict my freedom to pursue one or more of the options presented to me in a later stage. This is an important step, a kind of reality check.

I wrote at this step: "*Though I wonder at times whether enough is enough, I feel in my heart we have more than our share. Adds to the duty towards others to care. No excuse not to step out and answer the call*".

Step 4: My Being (Self Awareness through Skills, Experience, Values, Characteristics).

This step was crucial not only to the discernment process but also to the search for self awareness and provided a solid foundation for subsequent work on statements of personal values. This was an attempt to answer the 'who am I?' question along with enumerating my strengths and limitations. My preparedness for whatever outcome was reached in later steps was articulated here.

Careful review of the output from this step will reveal a general direction for the road ahead. It is important to be as objective as possible in this step. What others have said about me was important input along with what I had learned about myself from long experience with the subject.

I wrote in this step: "*I am much for to be thankful, with holes that could with work be filled. I must share what I am so that I might become all that I should*".

Some good background had been developed to this point in the process. However, I still did not have clear criteria with which to choose from the array of options that I knew lie ahead. The next step was to be the turning point for me.

Step 5: Decision Criteria

The need to develop criteria for selecting from a range of options was apparent. Having failed to receive a flash of divine intervention, I felt that I might be guided by those life choices that give me true peace and joy and so set about developing a list with commentary on the importance of each.

In developing the list, it was important to get beyond what I like to do or have fun doing. The notion of joy is different from and deeper than that of fun, just as calling is deeper than what one likes doing. This step required deep reflection. At the same time, it was accompanied by a strong sense of connection to a presence (I came to believe this was a divine presence) at a level that I had not previously experienced.

The result was revealing and surprising and included thoughts on my epitaph, adding further depth to my awareness of self.

As this step was initially done as a stream of consciousness, the list was far too long to be useful. By distilling the list through a process of combining like concepts and weighting their importance, I managed to reduce it down to four criteria, each weighted according to its importance. At this point, I felt a profound sense of accomplishment which seemed to indicate that I was getting close.

I wrote in this step: *"Four factors then, that's all. Amazing how it all works out. And I'm content that I have captured the important ones. Might this be God's intent?"*

Step 6: The Options

From step 6 forward, the process became both exciting and relatively easier. In this step, the options available, including my current work, were listed and each was analyzed against the four criteria in a straight forward, mathematical manner.

Each option was given a raw score against each criterion. Since this was not meant to be overly scientific, I used a simple scale of 1 to 3 with 1 a low score and a higher score better. The raw scores were then multiplied by the weightings and summed. My calling lay in the option receiving the highest score.

It is very important that this step be completed in the most objective way possible. Otherwise, the result may simply point to a new chore and not a call at all. It is very easy to under value the current role relative to the other options, particularly for someone with my penchant for change.

It is also important that all possible options be listed whether or not they seem whimsical or unlikely. This is an intense process and the result may surprise, as it did for me. I included an option that had been considered long ago, forgotten for years. In the final outcome,

it is always easier to criticize the known and glamorize that not yet met

this unlikely option became part of my calling. When you embark on this approach in a thorough manner, you never know what will emerge. And so it was to be for me.

I wrote in this step: *"Our present circumstance must be given the benefit of analysis most positive. For* it is always easier to criticize the known and glamorize that not yet met".

Step 7: Summary of the Call

It was important at this step to develop a summary of the call, bringing together the various strands into a role that is as coherent as possible at the time. Other elements that will contribute to achievement of the responsibilities associated with the call must also be identified.

At this point as well, another reality check should be done. Are the call and the expectations that attend achievable? Impossible? If the call involves more than one activity, are they compatible? Will any one activity overpower the others?

The call must be both internally coherent and capable of being done. And of course, the call must map onto one's personal values (an understanding of which was deepened as the process unfolded).

Once this step is completed, a period of deep, intense reflection is undertaken to provide confirmation. A sense of contentment accompanied this reflective period for me, providing the assurance that I was on the right track.

> **The call must be both internally coherent and capable of being done.**

I wrote in this step: *"There it is then. A role that I am uniquely prepared for, you see. One that may have been saved just for me"*.

Step 8: Action Plan

Knowing that I would be thrown back into the demands of my work and the chaos of my life back home, I undertook to develop the early steps needed to confirm my call with friends and family and to get a head start on implementing the new role. Included in this step was a list of people who would be consulted and those who could help.

This was done with full recognition that adjustments would be required as my commitment to this new role faced the reality of my home place. My sense was that adjustments are in the nature of a call, a realization that eliminated any sense of dismay at the prospect.

In the event, the importance of completing this step while in a space with limited distractions became apparent on my return to work as I had fully expected it to.

In this step, I wrote: *"While still in Durham, I'll begin a list of items needed and a detailed plan. Underway. Irreversible. Commits one to the path"*.

Step 9: Lingering Doubts

The final step identified doubts that lingered in the background and were bound to persist after my return home. In this step, I identified things that continued to bother me and those that I felt might arise later to shake my resolve. This step was a test of my commitment to the call and thus a test of the call itself.

The most serious doubt, "have I got it right?", was answered during a morning service in the college chapel shortly after the doubt appeared. In a short homily during the service, the priest officiating suggested that God did not care if we had it exactly right; close was good enough and we could count on help to fulfill our duty. This was answer enough for I was confident that I was at least close.

In this step, I wrote: *"My resolve must be firm lest those with good intentions shake it with questions, admonitions to continue where I am for the good of the community. Hard to resist, but I must".*

Final comments on my Durham time

The discernment process was designed and the nine steps completed in a two week period of intense reflection and Christian meditation with periodic discussions with academic and spiritual staff at the Durham university college. I admit to a great sigh of relief as the task was completed, accompanied by a huge feeling of peace and contentment and an urge to get back home in order to put the action plan into effect.

Where the time away is not available, the process can be undertaken over time with short sessions on each step. If this approach is taken, you might consider conducting it with a friend or mentor.

In the event, I encountered lots of uncertainty to be sure but not a single moment of anxiety. On return home, work on articulation of my personal values continued, work that confirmed compatibility with the vocation that had emerged from the Durham experience.

What was to be done at this point was to commit to follow the call and to get on with it, which indeed was what I did. My final words in Durham expressed the obligation that I felt from identifying my call: *"My destiny once discovered must be pursued. I have no choice'.*

ADDENDUM TO CHAPTER 11

Detail on the approach in the body of the chapter is provided in sufficient detail that further questions and clarification are considered unnecessary.

CHAPTER 12:

Durham Time Report

Why Bother?
(the major portion of my journal from Step 1
is included as these thoughts might encourage
you to embark on your own search.)

Why this quest? Why me? Why now, not before?
They ask, "are you not specially privileged?
Do you not have it all- good family, good job,
Respect, stature, profile, stability, peace and joy?"

Aye, in good measure have I gathered such blessings.
A good wife, too good for much that I've been,
Our kids all grown and fine people.
A job full of honour and worth with people I love,
And respect and the others you list. Yes, indeed.

Yet stature and profile I seek not.
They find me still and bring but discomfort,
For they raise expectations on continuous line,
Until tired, weary, burned out I become.

And a stable life was never among my aims
So no pleasure it brings to me.
Peace I have none, at least none in my soul,
Nor contentment derived from my now worldly role.

These things I don't seek I have in good measure,
Peace and joy that I need do not me much pleasure.

Lest you mistake my words, let me be very clear;
One treasure above all is my Martha, my dear.

These questions all cry out for response
So let me try to be clear on my reasons
For contemplating myself and my place right now
As I enter, in my life, the later seasons.

First, each of us must have a special destiny,
A call that gives our life meaning.
We must utilize what we are to the full.
We simply have no choice in the matter.

Then too, the times call for an unparalleled urgency,
As creation groans with a cry we must heed.

And my age, my energy both pass with time.
I can no longer say, "yes but tomorrow"
With any certainty that I will ever get to it.
[Note that this is not intended to convey that we should delay the process;
I am sorry that I had not initiated this at a much younger age].

I believe that if I discover and fulfill
My destiny, in that will be the elusive peace
And joy. I might even make a better place.
Discovery then is the task before me
That I must pursue and reach before I cease.

My Life Story
(portions of my journal record from Step 2)

Born on a farm of stable, hard working stock
Who saw family and work as the core of existence.
Taught love and morals, thought little
Of the greater problems of the world. Yet knew
The rhythm of nature, when the cow was due
And how many hens it took for a dozen eggs.

All the important stuff was there:
Nature, church, a judging God, grandparents,
Lambs, my own dog, and a fishing pole.
......

My life began to shift positively with Martha
Gently prodding and wisely counseling
That change would come only when I decided.
Right again. And finally.
......

I've learned from many quarters. Some lessons
Have stuck. Others have not. My kids taught
And tried. Patience. Tenacity. Flexibility. Forgiveness.
And now my grandkids. Curiosity. Play. Joy.
And above all, love. I'm learning.

Who am I? My Being
(journal entries from Step 4)

I am much for to be thankful, with holes that could
With work be filled. I must share what I am
So that I might become all that I should.
......

My integrity I value above all else.
By that I mean consistency, constancy. My response
To a situation is entirely predictable.
This I believe is the essence of a relationship of trust.....
......

An apparent, but unwanted, need for control
Means that I cannot bring myself to give over fully.
A heavy burden weighs me down. One I would gladly be rid of.
......

Honesty and hard work are bred in my bones.
Determination and diligence in difficulty.
Where others might give up, I persist. And complete.
......

Patience I have none. Impatient with everything
That lacks or is slow, not up to standard or
Sets sights too low.
......

A spiritual dimension too, scary to some.
Often appear inspired. Consulted on spiritual matters
In mentoring roles. Able to achieve a level of intimacy
With kindred souls.

And carry with me a naïve sense of wonder, of awe.
......

An adequate list, if it be true.
I am much, and me I must pursue.

Source of Joy and Peace
(journal entries from step 5)

My greatest joy comes during the things that I find least time
To do regularly. Top of the list is time with Martha.
Just the two of us. At the cottage. Driving anywhere.
Having breakfast at Erica's. Just simply being.
....

And then the thrill of achievement. I must admit to
The excitement of a challenge that has befuddled others.
It must be big. And important. I want
To make a difference. One that matters.
......

Utilizing all that I am. A challenge on the edge
Of my ability. I have yet to encounter impossible.
But when I do, I know that it will bring great joy.
The big one. One that only I am equipped for.
Fulfilling my destiny. Being what God would have me be.
......

An epitaph can often provide clues. To the person
Who there lies and mostly so if he has himself
Been the architect of the words. Let me try
With what I'd have them say of me.

This has evolved from 'here lies a decent man',
Through 'he tried to help' and 'he died giving'.
Now thinks me this I would prefer and ask
As I am carried to the place I'll be forever lying
You have these simple words placed on the stone,
'He never started dying'.

Making Sense of the Call (step 7)

Are we there yet? Me thinks we are.
The process undertaken, I cannot avoid the result.
Nor can it be negated or forgotten.
A sense of excitement accompanies the conclusion, though
No doubt that will ebb and flow as the work begins.
. . . .

So to my call to which in Durham I have been led:
"Care for creation in a deep, fundamental way,
Helping others see, understand and act.
Giving voice to those who have none, the poor and the trees".
Likely to involve active role in politics.

ADDENDUM TO CHAPTER 12

The importance of journaling is evident from this report which in its entirety ran to over twenty pages. Excerpts are indicative of the information that might be included in each step. Refer again to chapter 11 for questions at each step.

CHAPTER 13:

The Logic of Love

Arnold Toynbee said as his life's end was near that the purpose of human life is "loving, understanding and creat- ing" and that the greatest of these is love for it is "the desire that takes one out of oneself... makes (one) give (oneself) to

We cannot love what we do not understand.

other people, to the world". Toynbee has described the essence of a leader's role and obligation.

Inspiration emerges out of love (see Lance Secretan's "*Inspire*").

Leaders inspire. Leaders must love those who look to them for leadership.

We cannot love what we do not understand.

We cannot love another unless we first love our self.

We can only love our self when we have a solid understanding, a deep self awareness.

The first step in effective leadership is self awareness.

The logic is that simple and the practice is that difficult (paraphrasing Warren Bennis).

ADDENDUM TO CHAPTER 13

1. Do you feel inspired at work? To what do you attribute your feeling (inspired or not)?

2. Do you ever hear the word 'love' used in your workplace? Where is the word used?

3. Do you think love has a place at work? Why or why not?

4. Do you see the link between a person's self awareness and their ability to love? How about in your case?

5. How do you feel when someone says "I love you?"

CHAPTER 14:

From Cambridge With Love (from a long letter home at the half way point)

As I prepared for this experience, my prime objective was to refocus my life's work, to discern what I was to do for the next few years of a life that has less left than when I was fifty, to discover what service I was uniquely prepared for, to get on with the important work that would use me up, and in the process expand my personal self awareness......

I have always been comfortable with change, sometimes to the detriment of what is good about the present. I have approached the new with optimism and expectation and quickly grow tired of the status quo, easily bored with repetition. I have been called courageous and have described myself as having more courage than good sense. Wisdom is a goal and I sense that I am getting some....

A spiritual direction group is proving a serious learning experience. The divine is clearly present as we meet and my presuppositions about me are being challenged each time, a process both humbling and enlightening. I have carried a reputation as a good listener and try hard to be present to others. In this group, I have discovered that I recall what I have offered, when it is my turn to speak, with much more clarity than what they have said to me. This makes me wonder if the fact that I am more critical of myself than others are of me is getting in the way of accepting feedback as of any value. I need to listen, hear and accept feedback more effectively......

The message to 'step out' continues to plague me (reference an African American minister who challenged the congregation with "If you ain't stepping out, you ain't got faith"). Added to the notion of a prophetic voice (from a private conversation with a professor) and my understanding of calling as "giving voice to those with no voice" suggests an obligation that must be pursued. And the voice that said "you have already stepped out" complicates the question even further.

ADDENDUM TO CHAPTER 14

The entire experience provided additional evidence of the value of spiritual practice to an enhanced understanding of self. Some of the lessons:

1. Reflection on my attitude to change and the possible impact of my penchant for change on others.

2. The experience of a spiritual direction group, entered with some trepidation.

3. Reinforcement of my role in stepping out and speaking truth to power.

CHAPTER 15:

The Last Story:
Once More, Uncle Gord

My uncle Gordon Stewart was a funny fellow. Some felt he was at least half crazy. Even though often unemployed with no apparent resources, he somehow made a life. Always laughing, he brought joy to many. To others, he brought merely confusion or stress at their inability to see the joke that he always seemed to carry with him.

How can he laugh, they thought, in the face of so much hardship? How can he be happy with so few prospects?

As a lad, I not yet had the life experience to understand their confusion. I not yet had developed the level of despair and cynicism of my elders. I not yet had accumulated the wisdom that sees through the surface to deeper motives. I not yet had learned to even suspect that something lay below. I merely accepted what came along as alright, true, worthy.

So uncle Gord and I got along. I may, in fact, have been his favorite nephew for I joined not in the derision which came from his contemporaries. When he laughed, I joined in, for I found his laughter infectious. Not often getting the joke but that mattered not a bit. I had no choice but to laugh along with him.

In later years, I often wondered what it must have been that allowed him to laugh through it all. He had what many will call a hard life. Born into life on a farm, uncle Gord lost a son to suicide while my uncle was still a young and productive farmer. Having no other heir with the capacity and the interest to take on the role, he shortly thereafter abandoned the farm. Ever thereafter, he just seemed to float from one thing to another. In the floating, he alternatively sought comfort in religion or Seagram's gin.

My uncle Gord did nothing in half measure. When it was the gin's turn, he literally fell into the bottle. He had a measure of good sense even while under the influence for he rarely set out to endanger others. Rather, he would merely hide away during these times in his bus.

When it came time for religion to serve as comfort, he dived in with both feet. Uncle Gord's religion was seriously evangelical at a time and place where the norm was a conservative religious practice that makes today's theological conservatives pale in comparison. Confusion led to disdain and eventually to disconnection during his religious times. People could understand his enchantment with the bottle ("he lost a son, you know", they would say in forgiving him this) but no one could tolerate his religious fervor. "What the hell is he up to now" was a common query during the religious periods of a curious life.

Yet his life fascinated some of us younger ones. While many of the adults in our small sphere rarely saw the humor in life of those hard days, uncle Gord saw nothing but. We hoped that he had it right, that you could and should laugh even in stormy times, that there was always something to laugh about. It certainly seemed a better way than seeing the bad side of everything and frowning one's way through the day.

And uncle Gord and his various antics gave us lots to laugh at. He could laugh at himself and with us. So we laughed with him and at him and most often we did not differentiate. We just laughed.

ADDENDUM TO CHAPTER 15

Further learning on the value of optimism and laughter as a route through the more difficult situations.

CHAPTER 16:

That's a Wrap

Nothing much left to say.

Live to Lead. Self awareness is the missing link in leadership development.

As those who aspire to leadership roles become aware of the critical nature of self knowledge and seek out development opportunities that address this, the end result could be both better approaches to leadership education and training and better leaders. At the same time, those who have become self aware will be equipped to discover and pursue their life's work.

> **Self awareness is the missing link in leadership development.**

Better life leads to better leadership. The logic is that simple and while the practice is not easy, the potential for both life and leadership is only available to those who have a solid base of self understanding.

> **consistently asking the question "what have I learned of myself from this experience" is a sure route to a growing self awareness.**

Along the path, consistently asking the question "what have I learned of myself from this experience" is a sure route to a growing self awareness. The exercises and questions included in the addenda to each chapter are designed to encourage you to engage in your own process of self discovery.

The world needs your best and that is only possible when you know who you are and through that knowledge, what is to be your most significant contribution.

So, I urge you to pursue your self and leave you with one final question: *What have you learned of yourself from your reading of my 'who am I' journey?*

LIVE TO LEAD:

Selected Bibliography

(books that have aided my search for self and expanded my capacity to lead)

Emotional Intelligence

Goleman, Daniel, *Emotional Intelligence*, New York, Bantam Books, 1995

Goleman, Daniel, *Working with Emotional Intelligence*, New York, Bantam Books, 1998

General Reading

Crisp, Roger and Slote, Michael, *Virtue Ethics*, New York, Oxford University Press, 1997

Fox, Matthew, *The Reinvention of Work*, San Francisco, HarperCollins, 1994

Harris, Michael, *The End of Absence*, Toronto, Harper Collins, 2014

Palmer, Parker, *The Promise of Paradox*, San Francisco, Jossey-Bass, 2008

Scott, Susan, *Fierce Conversations*, New York, Berkley Books, 2002

Westley, Francis et al, *Getting to Maybe*, Toronto, Random House Canada, 2006

Leadership General

Armstrong, Steven, *You Can't Lead From Behind*, Calgary, Friesens, 2014

Bach, Richard, *Jonathan Livingston Seagull*, New York, Avon Books, 1970

Bennis, Warren, *On Becoming a Leader*, New York, Addison-Wesley, 1989

Collins, Jim, *Good to Great*, New York, HarperCollins, 2001

Irvine, David and Reger, Jim, *The Authentic Leader*, Sanford, Florida, DC Press, 2006

Kouzes, James M., and Posner, Barry Z., *The Leadership Challenge*, San Francisco, Jossey-Bass, 1987

Kouzes, James M., and Posner, Barry Z., *The Leadership Challenge Workbook*, San Francisco, Jossey-Bass, 2003

Kouzes, James M., and Posner, Barry Z., *A Leader's Legacy*, San Francisco, Jossey-Bass, 2006

Lencioni, Patrick, *The Advantage*, San Francisco, Jossey-Bass, 2012

Religion and Spirituality

Christian Bible, quotes taken from the New International Version

Brown Taylor, Barbara, *An Altar in the World*, New York, HarperCollins, 2009

Chan, Wing-Tsit, *A Source Book in Chinese Philosophy*, Princeton, Princeton University Press, 1963

Heider, John, *The Tao of Leadership*, Toronto, Bantam Books, 1985

Hoff, Benjamin, *The Tao of Pooh*, New York, Penguin Books, 1982

Mitroff, Ian I. and Denton, Elizabeth A., *A Spiritual Audit of Corporate America*, San Francisco, Jossey- Bass, 1999

Self Awareness

Keirsey, David and Marilyn Bates, *Please Understand Me*, Del Mar, CA, Prometheus Nemesis Book Co., 1984

Lee, Gus, *Courage*, San Francisco, Jossey- Bass, 2006

Lonsdale, David, *Listen to the Music of the Spirit: The Art of Discernment*, 1993

Olynik, Corey, *The Mentor's Mentor*, Calgary, Motivated Publishing, 2006
Palmer, Parker, *Let Your Life Speak*, San Francisco, Jossey-Bess, 2000
Secretan, Lance, *Inspire*, John Wiley, 2004
Stewart, Wayne, *Things I Know*, Calgary, self published, 2010

Servant Leadership

Autry, James, *The Servant Leader*, Prima, 2001
Block, Peter, *Stewardship, Choosing Service Over Self-Interest*, Berrett-Koehler, 1993
Greenleaf, Robert K., *On Becoming a Servant Leader*, (Don Frick and Larry Spears, editors), San Francisco, Jossey-Bass, 1996
Greenleaf, Robert K., *Servant Leadership*, Mahwah, NJ, Paulist Press, 1977

WAYNE STEWART

Wayne Stewart was born a farm boy with hay fever. His private sector career spanned 27 years throughout which he strived to build a sense of community in the workplace.

In 1991, Wayne began a second career in the nonprofit sector. He has served as the senior executive of three charities and as volunteer consultant and board member of many more. He has taught grammar school chemistry in England, leadership to MBA students at the University of Alberta, environmental studies to medical practitioners in Uganda and story telling to nonprofit studies students at Mount Royal University in Calgary. A strong desire to serve led him into electoral politics on two occasions.

Throughout his life, he has continually asked himself the important life question- "who am I?" and has helped many others with their own search. A life long learner, Wayne has degrees in engineering, political science, religious studies and philosophy and an MBA. He has learned from and been inspired by many friends and mentors notably Dr. Grant MacEwan.

His vocation is giving voice to those who are not heard. His joy and reward comes from those who seek his counsel and support.

He has been happily married to his best friend and constant source of wisdom, Martha Stewart, for over 51 years. Born near Dungannon, Ontario, he lives in Calgary, Alberta.

CPSIA information can be obtained
at www.ICGtesting.com
Printed in the USA
LVOW04*0234110216

474560LV00008B/34/P

9 781460 285466